UNDER THE RADAR

*A Memoir
of Musical Theater,
Broadway, Movies, TV*

by

Clifford David

Beta Books

Under the Radar, a Memoir of Musical Theater,
Broadway, Movies, TV © Clifford David 2016
Beta Books   ISBN 0-978-930012-54-0

§

Beta Books (www.betabooks.us)
is an imprint of Bandanna Books
for first and preliminary editions

Beta Books Titles

The Family Secret, Eleanore Hill
The Last American Housewife, Eleanore Hill
Period Pieces, Eleanore Hill
To Become a Landlady, Eleanore Hill
The Gingerbread Girl, Eleanore Hill
In the Aftermath of an Overdose, Eleanore Hill
The Martian Testament, Sasha Newborn
Eight 2 Two (poems), Sasha Newborn
Tanka Waka Uta, Hayashi (Dennis Holt)
How to Cook for Your Dog, M. Bowser
The Homed, a Love Story, Eleanore Hill
Corduroy Leopard, Eleanore Hill

The Bandanna Catalog

of classic and modern literature,
bilingual poetry, Shakespeare Playbooks,
argot dictionaries, gender-related literature
can be found at
www.bandannabooks.com

Contents

Introduction

Clifford David has spent over fifty years of his life on Broadway stages, especially in musical theater, in the movies, in a number of TV serials. A life member of The Actors Theater, he has worked with Lucille Ball, Marilyn Monroe, Richard Burton, Sir Laurence Olivier and other stars and directors. He shares some insights into the inner life of theatre, especially musical theater. You can see his impressive record of appearances online.

In this book, he shares the deep early life lessons that led him in later life to sustain such a public and successful career. These include his Lebanese grandmother, the search for a Christmas tree, the capacity for forgiveness, the taste and texture of the simplest things available to us all, the strength of family, and the inner workings of play production as seen in some of greatest writers, directors, producers, actors, singers.

Sasha Newborn
Santa Barbara, March 2016

So often we think we want to be seen,
and yet
so often we don't really want to be seen

The Dichotomy

So often we think we want to be seen, and yet so often we don't really want to be seen. Somehow that operates in a push-pull sort of way. So I'll take the liberty in beginning to tell that earlier part of my life as a prelude to the subsequent journey into the field of theatre, both drama and musicals, and to try to explain, or perhaps elucidate, what made me who I am today.

I believe that the early years form the adult and subsequent behavior as a grown man. What has an influence on how we see ourselves on this particular turning we call life, memories, or memoirs, of times past, and the people who would have inhabited them early in the beginning. Most family and friends have affected me and created in me my belief systems, both constructive and destructive. Yet, also has to do with the choices we make, what drives us on our particular quest. Senses, affective memories, both good and bad, have a distinct effect on all our choices.

Knew What I Wanted at Four

So, I knew from an early age, let's say about the age of four, what I really wanted from my life. Because my idea of playing, having a good time, was very often in the basement, dressing up in robes and ," performing plays, with some of the kids in the neighborhood that you could get to, follow, somehow, a storyline.

I knew somehow that I wanted to be seen as an actor, singer, whatever, but to be seen, to be noticed, I guess that goes along with what a lot of people do. And yet, somehow, trying to be seen, and not be seen, is that whole dichotomy that changes as you grow older and observe.

Different Choices

Along the way, others had different choices for me, as to what makes me, particularly, the person I wanted to be. At some point, someone decides that they want to be a star, that someone who is destined to make a mark in the world, first goes about it as a scientist would, that is experimentation. Trying, exploring, taking into account other theories that will ultimately act as an impetus to experimentation, exploration, to come upon a solution, a solution for a specific problem. And some, through that experimentation and search and quest, may even achieve a Nobel Prize for their work, and then, of course, worldly recognition.

Though, there will always be those who will tell you, "it can't be done," and whatever that is. It really just means to me that whenever somebody says, "you can't," what they really mean is, "I can't." So therefore, ergo, you can't. Well, if you listen to that, you're a fool, and unfortunately most of us get sidetracked or will listen to it because it comes from someone we think we respect, and ultimately, never looking at their own problems as the reason for their saying, "you can't."

So it was with me, to some extent, I was told that I was the wrong type, not the populous, or the popular kind of whatever, looks or behavior or speech, not quite aristocratic enough, or not blue collar enough. There was always something, and most people don't really know what it is anyway.

The Classics

So whatever aristocracy is, or is supposed to be like, from my earliest years, I can now tell you honestly that the classics have always been a source of inspiration for me. The choice was the classic kind of world, the classic in literature, the classic in music, the classic world as a whole, the art form, the way in which people ultimately strove their entire life to perfect whatever talent they possess, be it painting, singing, acting, dancing, no matter what. The classic world held an overwhelming fascination for me, and as I said both music and literature. Imagine coming into a popular world with a classic overview and then someone says that blue and white collar don't mix, I thought they did. "You can't," is a phrase used by those, again, who can't, ergo ,you can't; limitations imposed by others with a limited view of life and art.

Anything Is Possible

My view is that everything and anything is possible, it depends on the amount of work one is willing to make on behalf of that quest. I was more than willing, and against any odds that others may put before me, that others may perceive, I was willing to go the whole 9 yards. Again, it is in my opinion that it depends that in ones early life has had an effect, in every respect, on them, and how each one, each individual being, is somehow governed by what they see, what they feel, what they experience as a kid.

It has, at times, been a lonely road, hazardous even at some points. I believe that energy is closely related to creativity. I repeat that, energy, in my opinion, is closely related to creativity. The quest for whatever end is predicated on Herculean concentration, and there must be no side, no diversions of any kind, and that I where I failed.

There Are Secrets

Even though having achieved a considerable amount of success, that diversion cost me the ultimate prize. That prize known only to me, and one I am, and will always keep private. There are secrets each individual keeps for themselves and I believe, in my opinion, must always be that way, and must be kept secret. It does not enrich anyone, and it only serves as gossip for anyone who has nothing better to do in their lives, and at times, hence the reference to Under the Radar, A Memoir. What is important to me is how one's early life affects the life and the times of everyone.

§

My Mother

A case in point, as far as I'm concerned, is the effect that snow had on me. I was about fifteen when one evening I came home about 11pm, after having spent an evening with my friends from the neighborhood, I found my mother sitting at the kitchen table reading the encyclopedia, as was her warrant, very often looking up all kinds of information. She loved reading and wanted to know about everything.

Since she was married at sixteen, it was an arranged marriage, as was the custom among the Lebanese at that time, and may still be, she never really finished her education and she felt that she needed to better herself. So she took it upon herself to correct that aborted education, she read constantly.

There she was with this huge book in front of her, late at night. This all took place after we had our own house.

House Across the Street

We lived across the street originally in a duplex, one apartment below, one apartment above. One day my mother looked around and she saw this house across the street, a lovely house, as a matter of fact, my favorite house. It was a gray-shingled house owned by people whom had a factory down the block called "Ketchum's." It was her diligence and hard work and she said, "I want to have that house." She saw that house and it was empty, waiting for somebody, and that someone was my mother.

The house was beautiful, as I said, a two-story house, gray shingles, cream-colored trim, and a beautiful yard surrounding it. It had been built, as I said, by the family named Ketchum, who owned a factory down the street and produced equipment for automobiles made in Detroit, then they were assembled in Toledo or around the environs. She wanted that house, and she got it.

She did it by holding two jobs, one selling hats at a place called Field's Millenarian in downtown Toledo, and a factory job at the Auto Lite, and that was where they made generators and equipment for the war and trucks and alike, the time was 1944.

During the war everyone did what they could for the war effort, she was an extraordinary person. She was, never mind a woman, just fiercely patriotic. She had two sons in the war; Alex, a navy pilot; and Fred, a marine in the Pacific theatre. He was at Guadalupe Canal, Battle of Bataan, and all the rest, he was part of that first wave of marines that went in and it was extraordinarily dangerous. Both of them left the house on December 18, 1941, I'll never forget it.

Brothers

Each had volunteered in the service of their choice. Alex preferred planes, so he went into the navy pilot program, and he was an extraordinarily good pilot, unfortunately at some point during the war, you crash, and he crashed, and he lost part of his hearing as the result.

They rarely were allowed to come home on furlough, but our house remained open to all the service personnel, cousins, and friends of my brothers. My mother would get a call at about 2 am from a family member saying, "I'm down at the Toledo train station, and I'm passing through on my way, I have a ten hour stop over, and I was hoping that we might see each other." This was my mother's nephew and Toledo, at that time, was a huge train hub for the military.

Ultimately, she and my father would welcome them, "come on over," was the standard reply. My mother would cook and bake pies, at any hour of the day or night, so that the person calling could have a great meal in the warmth of family, no one has ever been turned away. On this particular night, she was alone in the kitchen, and there was always a pot of coffee on the kitchen stove. We were huge coffee drinkers.

Frankly, my heart went out to her, even more than usual, to see her working, to achieve a better level of education, and enlightenment. Her faith in herself and in her God was unbelievably deep and truly personal, a relationship that was unique for reasons in particular that I will leave out.

The Accident

Terrible things happened at certain points in her life, and when I was about ten years old, we went on a picnic. My father had a huge Nash, a big automobile, the kind that had two jump seats that came up from the floor, and as I said, we were on a picnic trip to Port Clinton, Ohio.

In the car was my father's brother, my uncle Andrew, and my aunt Ida, and his family, and all total, I think there were about ten in the car. Each had three children, so that's six, and four adults, so ten, ten of us in this huge car.

My uncle had two daughters who were twins, and my cousin Alfred and my aunt Ida, as I said, in our family we were five, my mother and my brothers - Alex and Frederick, and my father.

And so my mother had cooked up a storm, everything in the world that anyone could have wanted or liked was there, she made sure. Pots and pans were filled with every imaginable picnic fare, melons and grapes and every kind of dessert, everyone packed into the car. On the way for a great picnic day, summer was at its best, beautiful, clear, and sunny, a perfect day to have a picnic and to swim at the beach on the shore of Lake Erie.

Somewhere on the outskirts of Toledo, perhaps ten miles out of town, driving at a reasonable speed, since my father was not a fast driver, everything was going smoothly, when all of a sudden, on the front end of the car, the drivers side, there was a tire that blew out. My father lost control of the car, and as he turned into the driveway of a farm, the car turned, went into the driveway, and as it was wobbling, overturned, and the next thing we knew, the car was in a huge ditch.

Everything went flying, food, cousins, and all. My

mother received a concussion to the head and her kneecap was crushed. The next thing I knew, my mother and I were in an ambulance on the way to Riverside Hospital.

Injuries

I had a gash on my knee and my head and my back. My mother's condition was extraordinarily severe, so much so, that when she was taken to the hospital, they were afraid that she would not make it.

So, for the better part of a year, she was in that hospital slowly recovering, and then one complication after another occurred and she had a life threatening fever, and they couldn't figure out where it was coming from. It was then, and only my father and my uncle, the archbishop, were at her bedside, and I was there was well. My uncle looked around, and then he requested the attending physician to come to the room.

He said to the doctor, "You don't know where the fever...," and they said, "No, we don't really know. Everything seems to be okay, but there's something wrong, somewhere,"

My uncle said, "Of course. I would like you to take that cast off."

The doctor said, "Why?"

And my uncle said, "Because I think there's something wrong underneath."

"Everything looks to be perfect," he said,

"I don't particularly care whether it looks to be perfect or not, I want it taken off."

Well, being that he was an archbishop, and they knew who he was, they said, "Alright, but it's futile."

Discovery

So, they cut off the cast, and sure enough, there was this huge infection because the kneecap had been crushed and they had put in a piece of metal to sustain the leg, and it became hugely infected. The doctor said everything was fine, and my uncle knew it wasn't.

My father could've said it, but they wouldn't have paid attention because being a civilian, but the position of an archbishop was never to be countermanded; he said, "take it off," and they did, so there it was.

She was then immediately taken into the operating room, and the infected metal kneecap had to be removed and this enormous gash on her knee was cleansed and the metal taken out and another one not quite replaced at that particular time.

This all took hours, and needless to say, I was stunned and in a high state of anxiety and worry. The thought of losing ones mother, I don't know, fathers seem to be more replaceable than mothers.

After several hours she was taken into intensive care, and gradually the fever subsided. Had the cast not been removed, she may well have died and as I said, my uncle being a high-ranking prelate in the Eastern Orthodox Church could not be ignored, and he knew, he just had a sense that something was wrong.

The doctors were really astounded that my uncle would be adamant about it, and also that he had a sense that there was something truly wrong, and well, they were doctors, they supposedly knew better, and they didn't.

Eleanore

My mother stayed in the hospital, I believe a full year, and during that time the city afforded a daily nurse, her name was Eleanore. She came to our house everyday to take care of us, the three boys. I think it was through the hospital, or another organization, to avoid a lawsuit and to make amends.

Needless to say, Eleanore was a jewel. What a great lady she was. She could cook dinner for us, cook lunch, help clean the house, we all had to help. Each of us was assigned a room to clean or to mop or to do something. I always got the kitchen or the bathroom to clean up.

She saw to it, that our lives had some semblance of order because we were in school, and with my father, the three of us visited the hospital daily, to be with my mother. We just sat there helplessly, frankly, watching, but eventually watching her get better daily, and when it was time for us to leave my mother at the hospital, they needed to take care of all the medical needs.

Radio Programs

When we got home Eleanore had prepared dinner for us, must have been around 6pm. After dinner my father went over to my uncle's house, and the three of us would gather around the radio to listen to various radio programs: Lux Radio Theater, Jack Benny, Fibber McGee and Molly, The Green Hornet, and so many more things.

It was at that time my brother Alex would make fudge for us as a dessert and he would make the fudge into a thick, thick batter and then in this pan, a cupcake pan, he would put butter all through the whole thing, so that it wouldn't stick and then he'd pour the fudge into each of the sections that would house, normally a muffin, only this time it was fudge, and when it cooled he would just turn over the pan onto a plate, and the fudge would just easily and gently come out because the butter kept it from sticking, and then he would portion us our share of the fudge while we listened to the radio.

Frosting a Cake

One night Eleanore had made a cake for us as a dessert, and she said, "I think you'll enjoy this" and "goodnight boys" and she left. We all looked at the cake, it was beautiful, in a square pan, and we had a great idea, we thought, "Wouldn't it be great to have a frosting on this cake," but none of us knew how to make frosting.

After a lot of discussion Alex and Frederick thought, "listen, what could be so hard about making a frosting for a cake? It's easy! Just pour white sugar, about an inch thick, over the top of the cake," so they did that, and about awhile later, they'd look at it, and they said, "Well, let's light the oven," so they lit the oven. The idea being that the flame would melt the sugar and create a white frosting, this was their idea.

Now, I'm the youngest, so I just looked and said, "okay, fine they know more than I do, good, put it under the fire and then watch it melt." So often when a stove is lit, you can't really control the heat, they say you can, but this stove's temperature was hot. The cake, they put under the flame, and they hoped it would melt. And then all of a sudden, it didn't take long for the kitchen to become clouded with blue smoke coming from the oven. After scurrying to grab potholders and shut off the oven, they removed the smoking cake.

Right then and there was this sugar on the top of the thing turned black, lucky it wasn't an inferno. However, it was ablaze with fire, so much so that they threw a towel over it to snuff out the flame. The smell was awful, and once the ruined cake was taken from the stove, the sugar frosting had burned the cake right smack through, so much that all they did was open the back kitchen door and threw it out into the backyard. It was still smoking, and after the shock of this debacle we laughed until our sides ached, and later retrieved the pan from the yard, cake disposed of and the memory lives on.

Needless to say, such memories have a very special place in my life, and the love I have always felt for my brothers and my family. And that love takes precedence over any real hurt or imagined hurt and will always be deeply imbedded in my memory.

Never Walk Again

The doctors notified us, my father and all of us, they had warned us to be aware that my mother would never walk again, so get used to idea that she was going to be wheelchair bound and the concussion to her head was severe, plus her left leg and kneecap was so destroyed, that her body wouldn't be able to stand or sustain standing, let alone walking.

One night, my mother listened to all of us, and said very little, only nodding at the doctor, when told this awful news. We were all in a state of shock. How could this be? It was as if someone had punched me in the stomach, and I remember sobbing so hard that my mother motioned me to her side and put her arms around me,

I was, I think about eight years old and since I was the baby of the family, it was very difficult for me because I couldn't put the two together and I was deeply attached to my mother anyway. She assured me that it would be alright, and not to worry, she would handle it and everything would come out as God had intended.

Months passed, and the daily routine of hospital visits and, what, with school and Eleanore taking care of us, we tried as best as we could to lead a somewhat normal life. Finally, the day came when we were informed that my mother could come home, and the bedroom was prepared for her.

Bedrooms

Our apartment, our duplex, had three bedrooms: one for my mother, one for my father, naturally she had to be alone, and then the three of us were in the other room. So there were three of us in this one bed, I was always in the middle, and we had a big double bed. I was confined to the middle and Alex was on one side and Fred was on the other. Often, I would get out of bed in the middle of the night to go sleep on the living room couch.

After a couple of months with the arrangement, one night I heard some talking, and I heard this voice coming from her room, and I thought, "Who could be in there." So I quietly got up off the couch, and walked toward the bedroom door, which was closed at that time to keep noise to a minimum, and I didn't want to disturb her, but I wanted to know whom she was talking to.

So I stood outside the door, and I heard her praying, and her prayer was to the Virgin Mary. She went on talking to her as if she was just another person, and I wasn't sure what to make of this. Was she losing her mind? I don't think I had ever heard audible prayers from anyone, but I knew somehow it was private and I didn't feel it was right to disturb her or question her.

It became a nightly ritual, my sleeping on the couch and hearing her prayer to the Virgin Mary. Then, one night, I heard her praying and then, all of a sudden, stopped, stopped for quite awhile. I sat listening and I thought, "Well, she's through."

No. I heard this kind of rustle, a rustling of bed sheets, and I started to hear her, and I could feel the idea that, she was getting out of bed, and I wondered what was going on. So I slowly opened the door and peeked into the room to see her holding onto the bed, making her way to the foot of it, where she could hold on to the bed board, at the head of the bed. I heard her saying, "I will, I will, I will. Thank you Blessed Virgin Mary. I will, I will."

When she saw me looking at her, she said, "Quiet. Don't worry. Don't say a word honey. The Virgin Mary told me God wanted me to walk and she would guide me. So, I know I can walk."

"I Can Walk"

Well, all of a sudden the whole house was aroused and my father and brothers were staring at her in amazement. She said, in a strong voice, "I will walk. God has instructed me to walk." And from then on, we took turns helping her out of the bed, walking a few feet, until she had had enough, and then back to bed. This went on for a month or more, until she could move around the house with a cane.

The doctor's were absolutely amazed when we had told them what had taken place, "Come and see for yourself." They came and they told her that they didn't know how she had managed this, but it was a miracle, as far as they were concerned because they were profound in their assessment that she would never walk again. That the knee would not hold, that her body was practically crushed, and when they saw this miracle, as we all thought it was, they were astounded. Because, you see, the wound went from one side of the kneecap to the other and formed a very large scar that must have been about six or seven inches long, and about an inch, and inch and a half wide, and the kneecap seemed to be firmly in place.

The scar was quite wide and the pain must've been excruciating, and when questioned, she would say, "Soon it will be all healed and over with." Well, I couldn't be near any member of my family without physically feeling what they were going through. It seemed as if a thread of light was stretched to each of them, and never more so than with my mother. Her pain was my pain and her joy, my joy.

Decision to Leave

These were two of many events that have taken place to write about when that all of the thread of the events were a continuum. Events of my life and choices were formed long before I left home at the age of sixteen. At the age of sixteen I, with my elder brothers help, he'd taken me to the train station because I wanted to go to New York, and I went.

It seemed as if I had picked up all the choices and energy that I needed to go through this decision. My life seemed to be a ball of colors and intertwined, and the object was to separate, from this mass of tangled threads, the color that was me. I imagine a huge ball of mixed threads of color and then try to separate that one that is you. Often, one color would bleed into the other, and the pure color would peek out from only another, and I have recounted a few of the early years so as to show just how I was lead to make choices that often were not mine, but mixed up were other members of my family.

Occasionally, I was startled by what I perceived as being really me. Who was I? Who was I really? The discovery has taken a lifetime and the acceptance of what I believe to be truly me is startling and often dreamlike. What was it that I really wanted from this life, how was I to obtain it, such was my inner condition when I left to leave Ohio for New York.

I seem to have lived many lives, and the people I have encountered along the way are separate and apart, separate stories in themselves. Much like Canterbury Tales, a period of study in the music conservatory, a period of work in the work place, a period of trying to be an actor and studying with Lee Strasberg, and then as a member of the Actors Studio, and the long stretch of off-Broadway and Broadway, and the search goes on and on and on.

Never mind about the time, none of it meant much, what

happens to me is only important to me, and not to the rest of the world or the society I may inhabit in the future. Life can be long or short depending on ones will and, again, the energy that supplies the doing. You need energy always, as I believe, to achieve what you want to.

§

My Grandmother

To give the reader an idea of just how life began for me, I recount a story of my grandmother. From the time I was an infant, my mother and father kept house for my uncle the archbishop, and it seems that, just before I was born, my uncle sent for his mother, my grandmother, from Lebanon and brought her to our house, to my uncle's house actually.

She was the person with whom I spent probably the most time with, since my mother had so many things to do with the house, with cleaning and cooking and people coming and going and so on and so forth. It was from her that I learned my first language, which was Arabic. She taught me because she didn't speak a word of English, so it was from her caring for me, that I learned Arabic. It was the first language that I spoke, and I spoke it rather fluently and I understood her perfectly.

Since my mother's hands were full with wall-to-wall chores, my grandmother was basically charged with raising the three of us, and me in particular, and my brothers and me were as much a helping had as a mother could squeeze in. In Lebanese households, as with most Mediterranean societies, the family lived together all in one house, and it was full. My uncle would often entertain people from all over the world, and, naturally, my mother would cook for sometimes as many as twenty or thirty people, a regular guest at our house was Khalil Gibran, the man who wrote The Prophet, as in The Prophet fame, and I recall my mother saying that he ate little, smoked a lot, and constantly has Turkish coffee at hand, as well philosophical discussions with my uncle, the archbishop, was a constant, and it was in Arabic.

My grandmother was an extraordinary person, one whom, to this day, I see in my mind's eye. I had two extraordinary grandmothers. I never knew my fathers mothers husband, my grandfather, he died in the old country. I think that was one of the reasons he brought her here to live at the house, and a more beautiful person one could never wish for, she was just extraordinary in every possible way. It came to me that wherever she went, I went, she was, I think, in her eighties. Actually, she died at the age of eighty-three. I'll re-count the story, as I said-

Oranges and Rose Petals

Every afternoon my grandmother would take a nap, and so I would sit around waiting for her to wake up so that we could play together, and we'd have a snack and talk about all the things we wanted to do that day. It was rather different from my brothers because Alex, being the eldest, went about his business finding his friends, and Fred went off, God knows where, nobody knew what he did, only I, since I was the youngest I was confined to the house.

So I just sat around. I sat on the front steps of the porch actually and I waited, not particularly patiently, but waited for my sitto to wake up, sitto s-i-t-t-o, which is the Arabic word for grandmother.

This particular day was hot and the air seemed to be filled with water, as was usually the case in Toledo. It was not the kind that you could really see, but the grownups called it "humid." It was humid alright, I thought you could swim in it, it was so humid. Well, it was a good thing I had on my shorts on and a light shirt, short sleeves, and my trusty tennis shoes.

I always wore tennis shoes, to everybody's chagrin. I mean complain galore, "Why does Clifford always wear tennis shoes, why can't he wear shoes," and I would never wear anything but tennis shoes, except when I went to church, then I wore a pair of shoes, but otherwise I'd always wear tennis shoes. They would say, "Well they make your feet stink," and I would say, "So what. They're comfortable and they don't hurt or pinch my toes."

So, sitting on the steps of the front porch was kind of fun to watch the cars go by, and I would yell out, "that one's mine," to no one in particular it was just a game to see how many beautiful cars I could pick out and claim as mine. People walk very slowly because it was just too hot to walk fast, particularly since they would sweat, and I would say, "Hi," to most of them, because I knew them and I had been to most of their houses.

Why?

Any excuse for me to start talking, and the word "Why" was a constant with me. So then my family and my friends were careful not to engage me in any kind of conversation that might elicit a "Why." "Hi, how are you? Nice day. Hot," almost monosyllabic. "Where's your mother? Or your grandmother," could possibly take a long time to answer. "In the house," was too short and concise, when a long one would have been far better, and as far as I was concerned, that way I could have them for company for a longer time and it made waiting for my grandmother to wake up go more quickly.

You see, you have to once again grasp the idea that she was not only my grandmother, but she was my friend. After all a five year old does not have all that many friends, some playmates yes, but not really friends that could answer questions.

There were questions that I needed to know, and needed as opposed to wanted. Things like: where do oranges come from? What makes roses red, and where do they come from? How do clouds form? Why are some black and some white? Sometimes they're even pink or even red. Salmon wasn't a color known to me as of yet and after all, I was just five. So sitting on the front steps of my porch my mind was loading itself with "Whys," the need to know about everything.

Visitors

My mother, whom I adored, was always busy either cooking or cleaning or managing the house that could at any moment fill up with eight or ten people who'd come to call on my uncle the archbishop who was head of the Eastern Orthodox Church of a large diocese throughout the United States, Mexico, and Canada.

That entailed a lot of handholding and the care of delegates who came to confer on all sorts of things from petty squabbles to bricks and mortar issues, conventions, celebrations, funerals, marriages, the ordination of new priests and their respective assignments.

Time Together

Only the eighty-three year old grandmother had time to be with me and really talk to me. She spoke only Arabic and from that time on that was the only way that I spoke to her. I spoke to her in Arabic, as it was my first language and English came later. I spoke English to my mother and father, but to my grandmother it was only Arabic. English was with most of my family and playmates, but only Arabic with my beloved grandmother.

The times and days we spent together were always loving and filled with that special quality that happens between those who are at two ends of life: the beginning of the young life, just starting out on the journey; and near-ending that happens to all great, small, loving people. Sitting in the yard on a beautiful summer's day, eating rose petals was one of the special moments in time that has lasted me for my entire life. We would gather a few red roses from climbing the rose bush at the back of the yard, and they blossomed constantly.

Watching her all in black, as women of Mediterranean culture dictated when a woman's husband was dead, her hair was white and her dress all in black, against a backdrop of red climbing roses, a bower of green and red, and her skin was white and smooth, soft to the touch. There they lay, the roses in the palm of her hand.

She disappeared into the kitchen to wash the petals with my following her. "Why are you washing them?" and she answered naturally in Arabic, "Nothing should be eaten before it is cleaned." Therefore, she would take my hand, and we'd go into the yard where we would seat ourselves on two chairs. She'd then proceed carefully to detach one petal at a time from its place and she'd hand it to me saying, "eat."

I'd put it in my mouth and began to chew, she did the same, and she would look at me and smile saying, "isn't it good," and when you eat it, you'd become like the rose petal, on the inside of you, all silky and soft and beautiful. Beautiful, like the red of the petals, and it would give you a beautiful glow on the outside of you, just like all of nature...and that is exactly what I felt, all smiles.

After we had finished eating a few more petals, then we would play "catch the bird." Now that was a game that was played by extending my arm and the palm of my hand open, with the fingers outstretched, and gently she would say, "once there was a beautiful bird, flying around your open palm," the palm representing a bird bath, and gently she would curl one finger at a time to catch the bird in the palm of my hand. One finger at a time, and on the last finger the bird would inevitably fly off.

Not being caught, she would imitate the flight of the bird, up my forearm and tickle me in one swoop, tickle me under the arms and extended me so that my laughter would fill the whole place. Laughing and giggling, she would enfold me in her arms hugging me closely and kissing me on the cheeks, my eyes, my forehead, tell me all the while how much she loved me and what a good boy I was.

Naturally I wanted to play it all over again. The afternoon passed quickly at such times, and other times the day seemed to mush themselves into one long turnout sense of waiting for something to happen, something from the outside to shock the day into action, something to bring the squeal, the giggle of life tingling all over my body.

Shock

There was one such time, that brought a shock to the whole family, and I mean a shock, a real shock, all right. More like a cataclysmal personalities brought into violent collision with one another.

The innocent party truly unaware of the boiling pot, oranges are, and were, a favorite delicacy for me and was a feast for the senses: smell, touch, taste, and my grandmother knew this.

So, special times were set aside for this event. It was an event because it was not considered an ordinary fruit, it was not an ordinary orange, but the kind you might find in the most special of fruit stands or fancy stores.

They were very large, bright, orange spheres, much like the sun on a clear, hot August day. The smell had a sweet, piercing aroma, and when gently scored into four quarters, so that the skin would peal off easily, revealing the flesh of the orange untouched, like the yolk of an egg is protected by it's shell and the white of the egg, so too the white flesh under the skin was soft and spongy. The flesh when taken in hand, would come apart at each segment, each called a borg, that's the Arabic word for what we call "segments." This spongy layer under the skin was   there to protect the orange so that not a drop of juice was lost. Each borg had a thin protective skin, a veil, saving each teardrop of juice inside another, almost an invisible shell. Nature was an incredible packager of fragile, it's special.

Storing the Oranges

Since oranges ranked as jewels waiting to be shared by my grandmother and me, they were hidden from sight, and what better place than the coils of the springs under the mattress of my grandmother's bed. Large coils, spiral in shape, could comfortably hold one orange in place, protected by the mattress and the covers of the neatly made bed. There would be as many as three oranges hidden inside this particular package of man-made design.

When the occasion was just right, I and my grandmother would sit in the shade of the yard, she with a white linen napkin in her lap and a knife to score the orange, I looking on with excitement waiting with great anticipation for the coming burst of juice in my mouth that each borg would unleash. A flood of sweet succulent juice, my mind and body following it down to the pit of my stomach and my grandmother laughed with joy at my appreciation of the gift of the orange. I, being the baby of the family, received the most attention from her. She loved both Fred and Alex, but I was her favorite.

We were inseparable. We did so much together, took walks, sat and talked, played "Catch the bird," at rose petals and oranges, and at various times during the celebration of the orange my brother Fred would come into the yard, observing the two revelers enjoying the ritual of cutting and eating this highly prized luxurious fruit,

Fred came up at the last moment as the last borg was being consumed and he asked, in his usual brusque way, that he too wanted an orange. My grandmother said she was truly sorry, but that was all there was at this time.

Well, Fred was a very special kid; each of us was vastly different. Alex was sweet tempered, if you didn't cross him, and usually he could be heard coming home because he was always humming some tune or other. From an early age he was industrious and truly fun loving, nothing scared him and yet he was truly sensitive, rarely would he show his feelings. I, of course, adored him and wouldn't let him go once he'd committed himself to the suggestion of an adventure, when, how soon, it was put off for an hour or two, inevitably the wise would follow. Alex was always patient. Often he'd take me by the hand and run me really wildly down a few blocks to get me out of breath so that it would stop the barrage of "Whys," it was always fun. Alex was more a dad than a brother.

Fred, that was a different story. An uneasy truth existed from the very beginning. Fred was one of those people for whom the paradox of the ugly duckling turning into the swan was more than apt. As a kid the older Lebanese men would tease him and tell him he was ugly and where'd he come from and even more hurtful things were said. You see Fred had an olive colored complexion skin, piercing green eyes and kind of a blond hair.

When he grew up he was probably the most handsome guy anywhere, movie star good looks, women flocked to him everywhere. But, at this point in time, the time of the rose petals and the oranges, he could be ornery as hell and when he was crossed or denied what he wanted, he kept it away in the storehouse of grievances until it would erupt in an unexpected and, often, vindictive way.

New Shoes

New shoes were always a big deal and of some stylus concern; did they look good?; were they comfortable?; was the style right?. My uncle the archbishop had brought my grandmother over from Lebanon, as I said, and from a village in the mountains close to the famous Cedars of Lebanon and she came before my birth, and so from the cradle I knew her and could tell, even as a baby, who was lifting me. I could tell her smell, my mother had one smell, my grandmother had another.

From the earliest of times she spoke in Arabic, so as I got older there was no real learning to do. On the contrary, I spoke Arabic easily, and even thought in that language. It was English that I had to learn, and I learned it, basically, from an oral sense, and that came fairly easily. I was quick to learn almost anything.

It was not a question of what the color of the new shoes would be because there was only one color, black, and, naturally, occasionally white kerchief, or handkerchief, that she might put the shoes on just before dinner for the first time, so that all of us could admire them. She wore then briefly and then excuse herself to take them off and put on her everyday shoes, the new shoes were for Sunday dress only.

When she went to church, it had to be kept in pristine condition. Little things pleased her greatly and she had a sweet aristocratic quietness about her. She loved company and was enormously sprightly for an eighty-three year old. There was also something mischievous about her, modern, if you will, about her thinking.

No Smoking

It was a time when women didn't smoke, particularly in the open and particularly cigarettes, and the parish house, that I referred to, was rather large. It stood about three floors, and a basement where the storage of canned goods that my mother prepared some five hundred quarts of tomatoes and canned vegetables always on hand for emergencies and general household use.

The washing machine was also in the basement where the laundry was done, and this was before automatic washers and dryers. It as a Maytag that had a hand-turn roller on it to wring the clothes out, and my mother was immaculate in her use of that machine and the clothes that were white came out white, and her household on wash days smelled of soap and bleach and it wafted up the cellar door out into the open kitchen. No cooking was done to conflict with smells.

She was the kind of housekeeper that got down on her hands and knees with a hairpin to make sure that the dirt in the corners in each room yielded their unwanted dust and grit. The hardwood floors shown brightly, Persian rugs were set off.

Caught

A puff of smoke came up and he came down the stairwell only to discover two lady's puffing away on cigarettes. Caught in the act, they could do nothing but scream and laugh, smoke filling the whole room because it couldn't escape. I rushed to open the windows and towels fanning the air to expel the offensive smoke.

This, of course, was not the first time. It was mid-afternoon and no one was expected until 5pm. Only I was around playing in the yard and when I heard the screaming and laughter I ran in to see what was happening.

"Nothing, nothing. Everything's fine," came the answer. My uncle, all he could do to contain his laughter to maintain his dignity, yet his love for his mother and sister-in-law, my mother, kept him from a somewhat righteous, a somewhat feigned anger, and all he said was, "Aaib," a-a-i-b, meaning "shame" in Arabic, and tsk-tsk-tsk laughing, "Ladies don't smoke," as they put out their cigarettes.

Mother's Cooking

My mother, Lily, was a great cook, and as a great cook she could be found as great a cook could be found anywhere. Her taste in food and delicacies were renowned throughout the country and was known for her perfection, everything sparkled. My mother adored her, they were friends, my grandmother and she were friends, she was not just a daughter-in-law. My mother saw that my grandmother's clothes were spotless, always, and Giselle was her name which, loosely translated, is "Gisele," but in actuality it refers to the gazelle with its beautiful graceful lines and delicately refined relationship to the world it inhabits, she was all that and more.

She was born in a village in the mountains in the heart of the Cedars of Lebanon, but her soul would've matched any aristocratic society anywhere in the world. A meticulous dresser of course, all in black, her eating habits were simple, a little of this, a little of that, chewed judiciously, hardly revealing she had any food in her mouth. As for drinks, tea or coffee, but more often just water. Her skin was fair, even translucent, blue eyes, bone white hair that she braided and held tightly to her head, a renaissance face and demeanor that would fit any Botticelli, long tempered fingers held still on whatever she chose to do, sewing, reading, eating: the ideal grandmother.

Shoes

The next subject is shoes, and to be specific, my grandmother's new shoes. To add to that, is Fred oranges denied once again. Time had come for retribution. My grandmother always kept her shoes in their original boxes, old or new. One afternoon close to another denial of the prized oranges, my brother Fred had had enough. When no one was around, he snuck up to my grandmother's room and lying on top of the bureau were combs, brushes, and, like all, they were neatly arranged, and then he spied a glistening pair of scissors.

So, Fred took them from their resting place and went to the closet where her clothes and shoes were all neatly arranged, and there at the bottom of the closet were just a few shoe boxes, Fred reached for the newest one. Slowly removing the lid, wrapped in tissue paper, were the jewels, the new shoes- black, new, and shiny, beautiful new black shoes. The smell of leather was aromatic. He looked at them for some time, then deftly taking the scissors he proceeded to cut the body of the shoes from their soles that held them in place. Having cut both shoes, he replaced them carefully in their tissue paper and nestled them in the box that they had just been before. He carefully replaced the scissors on top of the bureau, closed the door gently after him, and when no one's around that afternoon.

It was hot and humid and steam just rose through and from the Earth and you could see Toledo was built on a swamp close to Lake Erie and gradually gradated into the lush and fertile flatlands that surrounded the city—it was not for nothing that Toledo's baseball team was called the Toledo Mud Hens, an apt name if there ever was one.

Fred closed the door.

A Car City

You see, Toledo, like Detroit, was a car city, and one car in the neighborhood, that belonged to a friend of the family's, was a real convertible, cream colored, huge in size, and a magnificent automobile. It was painted, as I said, cream, and it had two wheel wells on either side of the hood, and it was indented into the fenders with huge tires to match that were covered with cream- colored metal casings matching the body. The man's name was Tony Slibey, and he lived between Toledo and Mexico City, a very dapper man, sporty in every way, and he was to give me a ride, he always gave me a ride in it, as he knew how much I loved the car, and the ride was just an elegant, smooth ride, fast, and to this day, I drive only convertibles. Try to envision the early thirties, depression time, where strikes were common, workers against management, and there was a strike at the Toledo Auto Lite, which was a manufacturing company for generators and other such parts for automobiles. The factor was a few blocks from our house, and my father and I happened to be visiting a relative who had a home across from the factory. The occasion for the visit was to share wild pheasant, as he was a hunter and went pheasant hunting. Pheasant is a very special bird, and it happened at a very special time and season, I happened to be very, very fond of pheasant, so he made sure that I was invited. After dinner we sat on the porch, visiting, having a good time, until a fight broke out at the factory across the street. It seems management brought thugs to break up the strikers, and the ensuing results were that guns were brought out and many were hurt, and my father grabbed me and took me into the house to avoid being hit by any stray bullets. It was a rough time, humans against management.

I can still see the scene in my mind's eye, times were difficult, but it seemed Tony Slibey was not of the blue-collar working class, and he seemed to be doing well. I don't know what he did, but he seemed to be doing very well, and one day he was getting ready to go back to Mexico City, I assumed to do business, and he offered to give me one last ride before he left.

After this wonderful ride, he said, "I'll see you when I get back, and I'm going to give you something, and I don't want you to tell anybody. It's for you and you alone to keep and spend later or whenever you want," and with that—remember we were now in the depression time—he handed me a twenty-dollar bill. "Remember," he said, "Don't tell anyone, you have to hide it in a safe place."

Well, it is difficult to imagine what twenty dollars was worth at that time, it was a small fortune, and my head was spinning, not that I realized what a twenty-dollar bill was, I didn't, it was just a twenty- dollar bill. Where am I going to hide this fortune? I entered my house without anyone seeing me, and I started to search for a place to hide this vast fortune.

Our house was in mourning, at that time, for a family member who had died recently, and the custom in the Lebanese community is silence, no music playing, no dancing, no singing, no entertainment, at least during the forty-day mourning period. We had a turntable in the living room, and I knew that, at least for the next forty days, it would and could never be used, so I opened up the lid, looked at the turntable, and I saw that it moved, and I slid the twenty-dollar bill under the turntable.

Now, no one would ever suspect that it would be there, and if anyone came looking for it, they wouldn't see anything out of the usual, they'd see a turntable. Sure enough, Tony's sister, Ms. Slibey, came calling at our house, seemingly just a pleasant neighborly visit, and after all was said and done, she turned to my mother and said, "I think my brother Tony gave Clifford something, I think it was money, before he left for Mexico City."

My mother, not knowing anything, could honestly say she didn't know.

"Well, where's Clifford?"

"He's outside in the yard."

"Well," Ms. Slibey said, "could we ask him if Tony gave him something?"—that something of course being money.

"Of course," was my mother's answer. Do you know what it's liked to be grilled by a woman who's seeking money she believes that is rightfully hers?

I was about seven or eight at the time, and it was a time when tears could begin to flood like Niagara Falls.

"Tony told me not to tell anyone," I said screaming. It took some time, and quite a few threats, for disobeying Tony's trust in me, and remember, twenty dollars was a lot of money at that time.

Finally, I led them into the living room, lifted the lid, saw the turntable, reached under the turntable, and brought out this twenty-dollar bill. The inhuman cry that they let out was much like an animal screaming, "What's a little boy going to do with this small fortune?"

"Buy candy," I said, "and oranges," that was my reply. I'm not sure whether they hid their laughter or not because I was drying my tears and crying at the same time, and feeling like a traitor.

The rest of the morning is rather sketchy about this traumatic event, because the keeping of secrets is something that has lasted to this very day, a confidence that was once betrayed can't be corrected or made acceptable ever again.

Summer in Toledo

Some of the best alluvial soil anywhere in the world is found around Toledo, farming was a major industry. Corn, tomatoes, potatoes, anything that grew would find this soil willing to bring forth it's best, nothing tasted so good, so unadulterated as the tomatoes and the corn just freshly picked. Tomatoes picked warm from the suns rays and eaten just like that, no salt, nothing, just the tomato and you. Corn from the field to the pot with very little water in it to steam them, rather than boil corn, its sweetness was unrivaled, just the essence of corn and nothing else.

Skin white, roses red, brilliant colored oranges all to the touch and the smell inhabited my senses, both my grandmother and me. Times in the garden laughing, playing, talking, eating the fruits of the Earth, it was paradise. Sundays were for church, where mass was conducted by my uncle the archbishop, and everyone was held enthralled just listening to the stories of the bible being sung in Arabic in the Byzantine mode, his voice gorgeous, soaring, ethereal beauty unmatched anywhere in the Eastern Orthodox church, and the world for that matter. Worldly renowned packed into a beautiful jewel box of a cathedral.

People came from all over to hear the celebration of the mass as sung and preached by his eminence archbishop Samuel David. If anyone could be called a true Christian, more than that not just a Christian, but a humanitarian, a person who was not so specific to just Christianity, but to everything, to Muslims, to whomever, he was open-minded and inquisitive and caring and appreciated. Everybody's form and belief system and the way they conducted their lives and, as I said, their belief systems about how they function in this world- an extraordinary human being.

In preparation for church, great care was always given

as to how one dressed, particularly dressed immaculately, that is to be received by God in his house of worship so that it may be pleasing in his eyes. The house bustled with activity, as always, but more so on Sundays when the archbishop was in town and not at one of the other churches in the diocese.

That particular Sunday was the beginning of Lent, a time of great solemnity, as Easter was just around the corner, I was being given a bath by my mother, when suddenly a shriek arose from my grandmothers room, something awful must've happened to her for her to shriek like that, so my mother quickly pulled me from the tub, threw a towel around me and told me to dry myself while she ran to see what was the matter with my grandmother. Remember, I'm just about not quite five. I then heard another wail from the room, and this time, that came from my mother. With a towel thrown over me, and my body all wet, I ran to see what the matter was, I wasn't waiting to dry myself.

The door was open to her room, and on the bed the two ladies sat in a daze, each was silent with a look of utter puzzlement and, it seemed, quiet resignation. My mother was holding the tops of the shoes separated and apart from the soles.

Needless to say, the inquisition was quick and swift in its judgment. My father brought the razor strap out and he quickly put leather to Fred's behind, all the while Fred was screaming, "she never gave me an orange, she kept saying there was none, all gone. Except I saw Clifford eating one, and she kept them all for him."

Somehow everyone got through church, well ya know, they did, and Fred remained in confinement for quite some time. My grandmother was a woman of very few words and her way was simple and direct. No long face or disapproving behavior towards Fred, just an orange at his place at dinner at the appropriate time later. She never held grudges, the wisdom of the agent, not in general, but specific to this woman.

§

Wisdom: at Five Years Old

Spring is a magical time, particularly in those times that have a distinct four seasons. Forsythia began to break open from their shells, Pussy Willow, Daffodils, Early Iris, and the Flowering Fruit Trees, Michigan's sour cherries, the best in the world, apricots, peaches, quince, apples, pears, every other kind of flowering fruit trees, and then the lilacs, that was the signal that Spring was at hand, summer was soon to come.

Once again the time for roses and for the eating of rose petals and oranges at the side of my beloved grandmother. Five is an age where the world is being revealed in any number of ways. Women's dresses were thinner and brightly colored, men in white colored shirts and in time for white, white pants, shoes, shirts, Memorial Day. White and pink peonies, purple iris, violets, lilies of the valley, and huge beds everywhere filling the air with their incredible smell, unlike any other smell, it was intoxicating. I couldn't wait to pick them and bring them to my grandmother and my mother. Other than hugs and kisses, a true sign of love, and in my own way a sign of deep respect. A five year old has very little concept on what is masculine or feminine.

I was always moved by a spirit of what was, not if or maybe, what is, it's beautiful and must be shared, the sooner the better. Summer was a time for picnics and the Lebanese would gather from all around, even out-of-towners, and they would throw festival like picnics with wall-to-wall food. Music filled the air, dancing, laughing, all the sounds of life, swimming in the river, a very shallow river at that point, the Momi, food, you name it, it was on someone's table and everyone was willing to share.

Shish Kabob, Hummus, Tabouleh, Gousaf, Kibbe, which is fresh lamb made with herbs and ground wheat and spice, freshly baked bread, and Baklawa, which is Baklava or however anybody knows it, watermelon, every other kind of fruit known to man, and the ever present, Oud. O-U-D, that is this magnificent, like, half-melon, the forerunner of the guitar, half-melon shaped and it had all the sound of the Levantine world in it, plaintiff, mellow, heartbreaking. And then my uncle the archbishop would sing songs from the bible while the huge crowd sat around him, it was almost like being at the time of Christ when people gathered around, and it was a hushed silence, even in this huge space listening to the stories of the bible sung, as I said, in the Byzantine mode.

Emotions always ran high, some cried at the words and the melodies that came forth from this man, without doubt unmatched anywhere in the world, he was a master, and not just among his diocese but everywhere in the Orthodox world, in the Orthodox mass and as it was celebrated even in Syria or Lebanon. He was once a headmaster of a monastery in Balamond, in Lebanon.

Games and dancing came next and drums and the Dirbeki, the drum, as it is called, and line dancing, the usual line dancing that's throughout the Mediterranean, men, women, children all dance, though later would twirl a handkerchief or towel to denote the head of the line. The sense of that joy of living on this Earth was and is a gift, no matter what.

All cares melted away for this particular state of time and money, positions, society meant nothing, only the thrill of being alive and belonging to a world that knew your name, your parents name, even your ancestors name. If there was a time when the word "revitalizing" had a meaning, a true definition of what took place in this world, this was it, everyone felt renewed and ready to face the world the next day.

Not enough has been said about my mother. In my opinion, and in short, she was and is a saint. A person who gave herself unstintingly, she ran the bishops residence, cooked for hundreds of guests, cleaned, washed, brought up three boys, all of very different temperaments and different in every way.

Her story will come around at another time in full, concluding what can be said or confirmed as a miracle, and it happened to her at a crucial and critical time of her life. It was difficult for some to see life after this actually, and to be generous with ones assessment with the facts, but that is a rarified event for some....I belong to the "for some." The immense joy of just being alive and loving those in your life was and is viewed by me as a gift. How can there be such a thing as death? Who made it, and why? As for myself, the thought that anyone leaving me was unthinkable.

The philosophical view that immortality is in the remembrances of things past, people past, events past, mental picture of events that contained the complete sensory package, sight, smell, taste, touch, sound, the actual reliving of any event is considered by some as the seeds of immortality, that energy is all and create itself on another dimension. Ponderous questions that cannot be answered in fact by anyone disturbed me to no end. Not that posed such questions as a five year old, but I wondered at the disappearance of people and things.

Assim "Went Away"

There was a man by the name of Assim, for instance, he was a peddler who had a cart and a horse and he came three times a week with his horse-drawn cart and the cart was filled with vegetables, fruits, and above all debs, which is a molasses from grapes and it had been boiled down to a thick honey like consistence.

It so happened that one day Assim didn't show up. My mother, my grandmother, and all the other ladies on the block were waiting for Assim. Later I learned that God called him home, God called Assim home. I knew where Assim lived, just a few blocks from my house. Home? Assim lives over there on Mulberry St., so I went looking for him at his home. God called him home? Well, he wasn't there, because I was screaming his name in front of his house and no one came out.

I went in to the alley where Assim kept his horse, I really like Assim, he was a great guy, and I loved his horse, the horse was there, but where was Assim? What did God want with Assim anyway, especially on a busy day when all the ladies need to buy their produce for their suppers'.

There's the horse, but where's Assim?

The Neighbor

The next-door neighbor came out, she knew me only too well as the person with why why why why why why.

"Why are you crying," I asked her.

"I'm not crying, I'm laughing," she said.

"It isn't funny ya know. Assim's gone on vacation and Simha, that's the name of the horse, is all alone and the food is gonna get rotten, what's funny about that? I don't think Assim went on any vacation he's too nice and good a man to leave Simha all alone and go off with God. I'm gonna find out where God is and call him to bring Assim back."

The lady ran inside her house before she started crying and laughing and screaming so that I would never know how distressing this situation could become. I could talk your head off until I got an answer that satisfied me.

Sitto! Sitto! Sitto!

When I got home, I went looking for my grandmother, "Sitto! Sitto! Sitto! Where are you?"

Just then my mother came out of the living room. I was thinking to myself, "What's she doing in the living room now? There's no company here," the living room is only for company.

"Where's Sitto, I gotta tell Sitto I'm gonna call God to bring Assim back from his vacation because, you see, Simha needs him. And that lady can't take him alone, only Assim can, and the food, by the way, is gonna get spoiled. And also, it's Thanksgiving time, just a day away."

"Honey, Sitto went upstairs to rest a bit, so we have to be a little quiet," my mother said.

Well, I wasn't having any of that, I needed to speak to my grandmother about all this, and before my mother could stop me I bounded up the stairs and into her room, and there she was in the bed, propped up on two or three pillows.

I thought, "Boy, she looks white. She looks as white as the sheets," but there was a sweet smile on her face. The face was, in my eyes, was angelic and her skin had a luminescent glow and a smile that was reserved for me, usually. As far as I was concerned, it was like the sun and the moon got together to give a special smile for those on Earth, but particularly for me.

I said, "Sitto, sitto, sitto, I have a lot to tell you and I need your help."

She held up her ivory-like hand to calm me down, and slowly she said, "Alright eyenee," e-y-e-n-e-e meaning eyes, my eyes, "First we have to have a beautiful orange together and then we can talk."

I said, "Assim isn't here. The lady next door told me that God called him home, but he isn't home."

Go to Zouhary's

In Arabic, probably one of the most beautiful and flowery languages on Earth, she repeated, "Eyenee, you have to go to Zouhary's," that is the corner grocery store down the block, "Tell William to give you the biggest and best orange he can find so that we can share it together," my grandmother said.

Just then my mother came into the room. She heard my grandmother's request and she said, "Cliff," (she's the only one who ever called me Cliff), "Cliff honey, do as Sitto asks. Come, I'll bundle you up because it's getting cold outside and it's going to snow."

"Oh," I cried, "Snow for Thanksgiving, it's going to be beautiful. Snow for Thanksgiving. I won't be long, Sitto, I'll be right back."

"Wait," Sitto said, "I have to give you money for the oranges," and with that I drew close to her and she reached under the coverlet and brought out a small coin purse and she took out the change. This small hand was holding money and pulled me close to her and kissed both my eyes saying, "Eyenee ya eyenee," meaning my eyes.

I smelled her wonderful skin, and as I did so it was soft and warm, somewhat like the inner part of a rose petal. "I'll be right back," I shouted, and ran down the stairs and out the door.

It had started to snow and the ground became enveloped in a white blanket making everything look like a fairy tale. All that was ugly became blanketed in a kind of ermine wrap.

In the store William kept me busy. I rushed up to him again and again saying, "William you've gotta hurry, my sitto needs an orange so we can talk."

"You need an orange so you can talk?" said William.

"Yes. I have to tell her about Assim and God and how God took Assim on a vacation just before Thanksgiving when everybody needs him for the holiday."

"Alright, but I have to finish with this customer first, okay?"

"Please hurry, hurry, won't you?" I shouted all excited. It seemed to take William a long time, and I was running around the store going stir-crazy. It seemed to take forever and

Finally William came up to me and said, "Clifford, I'm gonna give you this orange."

My eyes opened really wide, "really?" I screamed.

"Wait a minute. I'm going to give you this orange for your grandmother on one condition."

"What?" I asked.

Bill said, "I want you to sing My Reverie for me." Now, My Reverie was a ballad loosely based on Debussy's Reverie, absolutely gorgeous, melodic song, and at that time I had a clear boy's soprano voice that had a clear bell-like sound the higher I sang. What a dilemma, I could get the orange free if I sing My Reverie and give Sitto back her money, but then again time, time was passing by and I wanted to go home to be with my sitto, what to do.

Bill said, "Please. It won't take long, just do the first verse, okay?"

"Okay," I said and I started to sing. When I finished Bill gave me a hug and the orange and he said, "tell your sitto hello for me."

"I will, I will," I screamed, and out the door I ran, snow was coming down hard and as it hits your face you can feel it melt and I was bundled up coat, hat, knit scarf, and boots.

As I neared the house, I saw cars in front of the house and I thought, "Good, company. And then sitto will come downstairs and we'll have a party. But first we have to talk, and she will tell me what to do about God and Assim."

I ran in the front door shouting, "Sitto, sitto, I got the orange, I'm coming up!"

When I got to the top of the stairs and looked down the hallway, I saw that the door was closed. I ran up to the door and started shouting, "Sitto, sitto."

The door opened slowly and I could see my uncle the archbishop, and another man with a white beard, something hanging from his neck, and my father and my mother, and they were all gathered around her bed. I could only see the top of her head, white hair, and it was my Sitto and her eyes were closed.

Sitto "Sleeping"

My mother was the one who opened the door.

"Is Sitto asleep now?" I asked my mother.

I saw my mother trying to hold back her tears and she couldn't, she could barely get a word out, and then she said in a very low voice, "Yes, honey. She's asleep."

"Well, when can I give her the oranges," I asked.

"We'll give them to her when her company is gone."

"Company? That's my father, my uncle the archbishop, another man, the only one who's gonna leave is the other man."

My mother wrapped her arms around me and held me close, "Just let Sitto sleep for a little while longer."

It wasn't until years later that I came to the realization that, simply put, my grandmother had died and she did not want her special eyenee to see her die. As always, she spared me the reality. After all, wasn't the world really oranges and rose petals. Hasn't it always been so in my life, in my young life?

§

A Shadow

On November 24, 1933 a shadow, really, a shadow crossed my mind. I could hardly believe that my Sitto would never play with me again, and every Memorial Day since that day I would take white peonies from our yard to her grave site, and when I grew older I had almost come face-to-face with death. Only that spared by my grandmother, she never wanted me to experience pain.

She died and didn't want me to see her dying. As I stated earlier, it is my belief that the adult that we become is very often, if not almost always, the result of those events, either joyous or traumatic, that happened to us in childhood, and I don't think that's a new thought with me or anyone else, it's been there and philosophers have talked about it endlessly.

Again, my grandmother, having spared me the event of her death, watching her die, is a generous thought in the extreme, particularly if you've loved somebody very deeply, as my grandmother loved me and I loved her. She was in my every waking thought, as well as my mother, but it was she, my grandmother, who often had a little more time because she was not encumbered with housework and cooking and washing and all the things that go to make up a life, so to speak, so that when my mother died, death once again entered my door, my entire world stopped.

Not only my world stopped but so had my entire family's world, and shortly thereafter her death, there was a gathering of the clan in the upstairs room and it was horrific, because behind it, behind all of it, lay fear and grief and mourning and also the pragmatic things that had to be attended to.

Mechanism of Life

What kicks into place is what I often refer to, to myself, as the mechanism of life, those things that make life go on, and among them the financial aspect of everything, in that I came from a blue-collar family. There was never much in the way of excess money, but that didn't stop us from enjoying life, having a good time, and loving. But when certain aspects of life take hold, and they intrude on the modus operandi of the day, there is that business of death in America has become such a financial obligation, the kind of casket that one has, the color it must be, and who's to do what, and who's to pay for what, but underlying it all in my mind was the shame of what it was all about, the death of one incredible woman, one who in life seemed fearless.

If anyone tries to explain the human condition and what family, love, hatred, rage, anything about the human, is absolutely daunting, if not an impossible, task. The person or persons in your family that you love unconditionally can at crucial moments so disappoint and scare you that you must tell your mind that you really do love them, that there are parts of that person, brother, wife, mother, that is shattered at that moment.

An insufferable pain courses through your body, through my body, as it did, the acting out of each member of the family, what is required, what seems good, what is right, what what what, it aches to think about it, it even aches to write about it. You can write or say all you want about us as human beings, but the plethora of writings and discussions about "We stink, we're a jealous bunch, we hate with all our souls, we're a bunch of filthy liars hiding behind masks of deceit, we're killers every one, we lie, cheat, steal, swindle, in short we're a rotten bunch."

Then comes along these exceptions and I changed my mind.

Those who surmount every possible odd, whose generosity and compassion swells your heart and brings tears to your eyes. But is greed everywhere? If it's everywhere, how come a few escape and rear their almost divine heads, you figure it out.

Somewhere there has to be a motive, an aberration in the structure of the genetics that make up these individuals. Why? It's a tiresome exercise and great philosophers have had their minds on it for centuries past and present. Still, it is an unanswered question for most of us.

§

A Drowning: Age 10

As I said, what happens to us in life early, affects us later, even though we shove it under the proverbial rug it's somewhere in there, everything is in there, we are extraordinary in our ability to remember and to feel.

The day was sunny and humid, as always, and there was a river by our house, the Momi, that was inviting and absolutely forbidden by any parent within miles of the river's edge, "Don't go near it."

It wasn't a very pretty riverfront, railroad tracks, rundown warehouses, weeds, sand dunes that reached way into the sky 30-40-50 feet, and the river, worst of all, was the color of mud, muddy yellow with all the flotsam and jetsam floating on its surface, all shapes and colors interspersed but floating condoms from last night's desperate search for what we call love, and in most cases it was, to use an impolite word, just fucking and more likely to be discussed in school the next day, who put out and who didn't, maybe a pregnancy and an ever long, dragged out road of pain for the individuals. Not nice words, but that word particularly of filth, the intent of that act without commitment or true love boggled most cases, nature at work and who said nature was kind or even feeling.

Again, like all of us, it's a bundle of paradoxes, beautiful, breathtaking, yes, breathtaking even, nature at work creating new lives, new species, new complexities to puzzle the world. Hot doesn't describe the air in Toledo at that time, humid, even if it clings to your clothes and skin, still doesn't describe it. To the very marrow of your bones in your body I have a sickness, and it swells inside of you and makes you feel sick with sex, sex ever constant in all the places that nature has provided for procreation and sadistic fun.

Watching Billy Drown

There was a day a group of boys, aged eight to twelve, a bunch of us went down to the river, unfortunately we didn't know what was to happen. What we did was watch a friend of ours drown.

We watched Billy, that was his name, Billy, drown.

We didn't have any idea that this could conceivably happen, but did it just happen?

The mother screamed through the neighborhood that he was pushed, Billy an eleven-year-old was pushed by one or more of the boys in the neighborhood, not true, and it was also bad enough that her husband, a construction worker, fell to his death from a huge construction job downtown just two days later, she went out of her mind—who wouldn't, how much can a person take?

The road to poverty and pain is covered with such events, the scarring of the psyches of the boys involved, all of us, took greater or lesser degree depending on the sensitivity of each of us, for it was a killer, a thought of punishment and guilt had sown the seed firmly implanted in every part of my being, seen and unseen. I stood at the corner of River Street, looking down in all directions, looking just to divert my mind on the license plates of oncoming cars as they whizzed passed, Illinois, Indiana, Texas, what are they doing up here, Kentucky, West Virginia, Pennsylvania—no, Massachusetts.

What actually happened was that the fire department somehow was notified and some of us were just standing immobile, and I remember distinctly a fireman kind of shaking me a bit out of this kind of mesmeric stupor. I couldn't believe what I had just seen.

Billy had just slipped, I don't know how, went down in the water once, came up twice, came up a third time, stayed down. Well, fear riddled my body, and I thought, "Oh my

God, how did this happen?"

So, after I was shaken out of this state, the only thing I could think of was to go sit by the side of the road and to watch cars pass, looking at license plates and then hoping that it would—well, I don't know what I was thinking of frankly, I just thought, "Well, I'll look at license plates." Massachusetts, that's where my grandmother and another grandmother, and my aunts and uncles, and the entire adult family lived, and I thought, "Well, why aren't they coming?."

They come during the summer to visit, and our house bulged with everyone cooking, yelling, teasing each other, laughing, a whole array of human emotions filled our house and the number who came from these places varied from four to six, and some would stay with my parents and some with our other relatives and they would converge at one house or the other and the visit usually was a prelude to a big festival given by the church, a kind of conference and a time of remembering where they had all come from, their descendants, their parents had all come from Lebanon with nothing.

The church was filled to overflowing and spilled out onto the sidewalks. Everyone dressed-to-the-nines, it was a time of worship and play, a time of singing, dancing, eating, and a time to hear mass again sung by my uncle and his marvelous Byzantine-style of singing, it was, as I said, intoned by the world's most foremost exponent of ecclesiastic singing.

People would come from all over the world to hear Archbishop Samuel David conduct a three-hour, four-hour Eastern Orthodox mass. I was an altar boy at the service of my uncle. The pressure and responsibility of being the arch-bishop's nephew was a tough one, you were supposed to set an example for every other kid on the block and every kid everywhere, Mr. Perfect, sweet Mr. Perfect, kind Mr. Perfect, understanding and sympathetic Mr. Perfect, in short, the Messiah resurrected on his way to being a priest, and then a bishop, and then possibly a metropolitan archbishop—and I was only nine or ten at the time. Who knew what lay ahead?

The day was a cold one, November 23rd, in Ohio and the wind swept over the city coming from Lake Erie. Lake Erie was cold, freezing, and filled one with just enough moisture, the wind, to slice through your body, and the windows of the house steamed up from all the cooking, getting ready for Thanksgiving in our house, actually my uncle's house, the Parish House.

My parents and my brothers lived there for quite some time. We were three boys three years apart, my uncle, the Archbishop, my grandmother—my uncle brought his mother, brought her over from Lebanon seven years back.

A Summer's Day

On a summer's day, my grandmother and I would sit in the yard, and there was this special mixture of yogurt and cracked wheat that is made rolled into small balls and laid out on a white sheet, usually on a long table, laid out to dry over the tabletop. And in this large bowl of yogurt and wheat, having been mixed a little at a time, she'd dip her hands into the bowl and bring out just enough for the mixture to make these small marbles of yogurt and wheat, and then as they would dry and the sun would beat down on them, she covered it with a gauze so that flies or anything wouldn't get on them. And then she'd just sit by and fan the air so that nothing would disturb it, and then once they were dry, they were mashed into a coarse powder and stored in jars for the winter. This mixture, once dried, provided a base for all kinds of cooking—soups with chopped lamb and nuts, small tortellini-like puffs stuffed with herbs thrown into this boiling soup. It's a very ancient dish that provided all the nutrients needed for a strong, healthy body, not unlike the Kurds who eat yogurt and dried apricots as a daily diet.

When the task was finished and these balls of yogurt were laid out on a table, it reminds me of looking at those candy strips with little dots on a strip of paper, it kind of reminded me of that.

My grandmother always wore black, but only on this day she had a huge, white spotless apron wrapped around her, and her pristine head, a white head-handkerchief to cover her hair. She was immaculate about her person, and never more so than when she was cooking. When her work was finished, she'd go into the house and clean up, and then she would return to the yard, see that all is well with her preparations, then this gauze would gently be removed, as they were dried, and then she would put it all together and let it mash into this granulated, well it looked like sugar, then she would bring a chair into the yard, brought out from the kitchen, and sit down in it, then she'd get up and go to the rose bush, pick some beautiful red roses, the climbing ones, and then she would call me to come and sit with her while we watched the food drying. She then did something that I had never seen done before, she began to pick the petals of the roses off of them and put them in her mouth to chew.

A kid doesn't see anything unusual in this act, and when she asked me to eat some of it with her, I did. She told me in Arabic to think of color as the taste when I chewed the petals, to feel the perfume of these very fragrant roses in my mouth and the sweetness of the smell as I chewed them. It was wonderful, a hot summer day sitting with my beloved grandmother chewing rose petals as we watched the sun beat down on the table waiting for the yogurt to dry.

The early times were hard, they were good and hard, they were hard and good, and I was completely aware of everything around me from the earliest age, the smell of our house, the colors around me, literally the vibrations of each person, sometimes so aware that it became painful—was everything all right, how'd the people around you feel, were they smiling, laughing, angry, or intensely fuming. The fear of just about everything that seemed out of balance, a totally unrealistic approach to life, but when you're a kid it's so important for you to feel safe.

Sense of Fear: Nineteen

I think I can pinpoint the first time I had a deep-seated sense of fear, fear in a blinding flash which has lasted to this day, each day had, and has, a quiet form of appreciation, apparition, call it what you will, "just keep the boat steady" is the mantra of my mind. It was a winter night and I was visiting my home in Toledo for the holidays.

You see, New York was my home, transplanted home now, and Toledo was where I was born and grew up until the age of sixteen, and it seems that I was about nineteen at this time, and there was something so soothing and complete about winter and the snow covered the ground, a cocoon of sorts. I came in the side door kicking off the snow from my shoes, and I heard my mother call out to me, "is that you Cliff?" No one but my mom ever called me Cliff.

I answered, "Yes mom, it's me." I went into the kitchen and found her sitting alone at the kitchen table, it was about 9:30 pm,

"You're home early," she said.

"Yea, I just had an urge to be home. Any coffee?"

She said, "I just made some." Well I had an urge to have some right then and there. She said, "I'll get it."

And I said, "No, no, you've waited on everyone much too much."

She looked okay, but I knew she was tired from an exhausting day working downtown selling ladies hats to crowds of women—hats are not a common item in today's world. And then she'd cook dinner for all of us, me, my father, my two brothers, we were five. Now we were no more but one, me.

A deeply affecting situation to be the last one, so easy to lose perspective on life and yet I must say I was keenly aware of my relationship to every member of my family. Their love and support meant the world to me, my world.

My mother sat at the kitchen table with the coffee in front of her; the kitchen was warm and had a wonderful smell, as it always did. My mother was a great cook, and I use the word advisedly, great in that she cooked dishes that were considering the best of Arabic cuisine. As you well know, Arabic cuisine comes from the Ottoman Empire and nothing was spared for that kind of cooking, that cuisine—light, delicate, truly flavorful with spices that are very, very special. People continued to call on her for her recipes and help with the big church functions given by the ladies club, of which she was president.

I poured my coffee and sat across the table from her, her face was a beautiful one, a beautiful one in the biblical sense, Semitic eyes, deep and thoughtful, and above all forgiving in everything she saw and every action by anyone. She could only see the good in people, she made excuses for everyone no matter how hurtful or insensitive their behavior might have become.

There was something so child-like in her behavior and joy of life. Her laugh was full and yet delicate at the same time. Conversations between anyone are often strained and guarded in a way that is really not discernible; rarely do people open up their hearts and minds to one another.

Opening one's self up, and opening up their sense of need, a need of one's stirring, invigorating, erupting until an understanding is, for the moment, achieved—it's like listening to music that seeps into every pore, filling you with sheer sound, snow was like that for me, as well as music.

My mother asked me how I was, and was I happy being home for the holidays, it was Christmastime.

I answered that it was good to be home and living with the family, all of us, and the many friends I went to school with. As the conversation progressed between us, I noticed a slight sadness about her, and asked her, "Are you alright?"

She said, "yes." That was the only thing with my mother, and it isn't until later in life that you realize that your mother had, or has, a mother, and that the need to communicate with her is just as needful as ours is to be heard by our mothers.

Recurring Memory

I had had a recurring memory of an event in my life that I often wanted to confirm or talk it up as a fantasy or imagination in the extreme. I heard myself say, "I have something I want to ask you about."

She looked at me, not sure what it was that I wanted to ask.

I said, "I remembered something, and I want you to tell me what it is."

She took a sip of her coffee and she said, "I'm listening."

I said, "Well, I seem to have a memory of something that happened, I believe, a long time ago," I went on, "and I can't place any of it. Let me tell you this, I remember a cold, wet feeling hitting my face, and I see a dark figure helping someone down with what I now know were steps. Two children were helped down as well as myself, and it was dark outside and I feel as if I'm wrapped in something and this person is carrying me in her arms with only my face exposed, feeling this cold, wet something hitting my little face. Does any of this make sense to you?"

A long silence ensued, and I wondered why it took so long for her to answer, and then in a small voice I heard her say, "Where did you hear that story?"

I answered, "I didn't hear it, it's something that just pops up from time to time, and I want to know if you know anything about it,"

Nothing was said for a long while, I just waited. And then she raised her eyes and faced me and said, "Very strange, you were only three or four months old, and you can't remember anything like that."

"But I do," I insisted, "Something happened, I see it clearly in my minds eye, I can see it now if I choose to remember."

My mother said, "But Cliff, you can't, somebody must've

told you something about it."

I said, "No. No one told me anything. There are many things I remember very clearly from all ages of my life, so please, tell me what this particular event is that I remember,"

And slowly she began to tell me this story of a trip she had taken with the three of us to see her mother in Worcester, MA. Along the way, somewhere along the trip, Buffalo, NY or something like that, the conductor asked her for the rest of her ticket to Worcester. She told me that she only had enough money for part of the way and the moment had come for her to admit that she had only purchased part of the ticket to Worcester because she didn't have the money for the rest. As hard as it seems to realize, but in fact it did happen, the conductor pulled the cord for the train to stop somewhere in the countryside. It was black out and the only lights around us were the lights from the railroad car.

She then recounted how this person, this conductor obviously, helped us down out of the train, out on the stairs with all of us, and she crying and begging for us not to be put off. It was snowing out, not heavily, but lightly. We stood out there for a while, I'd imagine with me in my mother's arms, and my brothers crying as well. She then said someone on the train talked to the conductor, and he said it was his way of deterring others from doing the same thing at another time.

Finally, we were helped back on to the train to complete the trip to our grandmother's.

I sat dead still, I could see that she was very close to sobbing, not crying, sobbing, something she rarely did. Her heart was breaking as she realized that somehow I knew an awful event in our lives, difficult though it may be to comprehend because I was just a baby, but it was part of a nightmare, and that it still astounded her that a four-month-old baby was that aware of sight, sound, sensations surrounding events in life, not yet old enough to comprehend anything, or so she thought until now. I think somehow we now know that babies know far more than we are willing to admit or comprehend.

My mother and I sat silently for a long time, and then I reached my hand across the table to hold hers, it was a touch I shall never forget. Life had been hard for her, with few rewards, except praise from loving admirers and acknowledging the extraordinarily good woman that she is and was.

Arranged Marriage

As for marital love, that was something foreign to my father and his entire generation, matched marriages only aspired to a kind of compatibility and consent that two could, and these are my quotes, "get along."

My mother came from a large family of seven   children, in which my mother was next to the youngest.

My father came from an equally large family, all born in Lebanon, and there was one very distinguished brother in his family, that had a glorious voice, and at an early age was sent to a seminary to study for the priesthood. It seemed in those days in Lebanon, or in the Near Eastern countries such as Lebanon, that if a male had a good voice, he was sent into the seminary to see if such a boy could be developed into a priest, and if he chose to remain celibate, he could attain a position of great prominence, be it archimandrite, bishop, metropolitan archbishop, and with fortune, he may even become a patriarch in the Eastern Orthodox church.

Voices were one way to obtain status and recognition since the literature is sung, the bible is sung according to the strict Byzantine tones and rules. Nothing was written down, it was passed down in oral tradition, they were set in tones and the melody or chanting was left up to the musical skill or vocal inspiration of the priest.

It just so happened that my uncle was both vocally and intellectually superior to anyone that had come along in a very long time. It also helped that there had often been at least one male member of our family who had been priests, members of the Husum family, or David family, as we were now known.

That lineage went back five or six hundred years, the family could trace members of their family who entered the priesthood for centuries, but it was my uncle, the archimandrite, at that time who, as acting head of the family in America, approached my grandmother Rose and my grandfather Peter, my mother's father and mother, to see if a match could be made for his brother Ferris with their daughter Lily. I was told there were several family gatherings with everyone in attendance from both sides.

In the little towns of the entire Mediterranean, including Sicily, Cyprus, Malta, they still hold to this custom of matched marriages. It was during these get-togethers that the two intended members would see if a match was possible, and, if it were agreed upon, then a wedding would take place. It was a highly desirable match, in our particular society, to be married into a family as prestigious as my father's family, particularly since my uncle was already renowned in the most important way of all family life among the Lebanese: the church.

All life revolved around the church, weddings, funerals, picnics, dinners, seemingly, and maybe in fact, tribal in every respect. It was an honor to have my uncle as a guest and every member connected with his family was equally honored with preferential treatment everywhere, and I mean everywhere. It was akin to royalty in this particular society, and also the added advantage that his voice was so extraordinary, as I said, people flocked to hear him conduct mass.

The Orthodox mass lasts about three hours, three sections of the mass were conducted one after the other and not divided as in the Catholic church—early mass, high mass, and low mass.

My mother was sixteen, my father thirty. My father had come over on a boat from Lebanon at the age of eleven with a tag around his neck, got off at Ellis Island and was met by one of his older brothers who had preceded him by about five years. He was brought to Springfield, MA where his three older brothers lived; they were peddlers who went from door-to-door selling small household items, thread, buttons, pins, etc. Eventually they saved enough money to open a dry goods store.

My uncle was elevated to archimandrite while serving under his mentor, archbishop Victor of Worcester, MA, and that is how he met the Abnou family, my mother's maiden name, and how he came upon the idea that his brother Ferris and my grandparents daughter Lily might make a good match.

Early Family Life

My mother and I held hands for quite a while, nothing needed to be said, I could feel deeply all the disappointments of her life, I'm sure there were happiness's as well as sadnesses.

I remember our early life as it happened. My mother and father eventually moved from Chicopee, MA to Toledo to live with my uncle the archbishop, and my mother then assumed the position of cook, housekeeper, general caretaker of the parish house, a fancy name for a very nice but ordinary house on Magnolia St., 624 Magnolia to be exact, smack in the middle of the Syrian/Lebanese community.

St. George's Cathedral was just a few blocks away, that was my uncle's diocese; my father obtain a civil servant's job as a rotor meter reader and a city job with steady and respectable pay. It was there that my mother cooked for hordes of visiting dignitaries who came to discuss church matters and feast on my mother's incredible Arabic cuisine.

Some dishes had a history that dated back a thousand years or more, some were highly complicated requiring days of preparation, and some very plain and simple, yet elegant food, breads, which she baked, of all kinds, and desserts, one even more exquisite than the next, hard work at any rate, but one which seemed to give her pleasure.

She adored my uncle, as he adored her for the mother and wife she was to his brother. He made sure that she was respected and appreciated by all who came to our house, enough to say he was uniquely a spiritual man and one whose dedication to his church was complete and without the power-hungry aspects that so inflate many who attain high-authority in a church or in any church.

He was the people's priest, who cared for them and saw that those who had little were helped with the essential needs, food and clothes, and when they came to church he instructed them to give very little. Once around Easter-time when the clergy went around to the houses of the parishioners to bless them with holy water, as is the custom in the Orthodox Church, he visited a house with a widow and three children and told her not to give anything.

My mother and I sat there in the kitchen, for a rather long time not saying a word, I became embarrassed for having opened the door on a past that had been better left unsaid, unopened, but I have always been one to ask why—why became a way of life for me, and always will be, with greater or lesser reasons to know.

The Movies: Eleven Years Old

It seems that my life and events continue to flow in and out of my mind, pictures fully developed in living color. The snow was falling and the night was dark, only lit by the refraction of the streetlights bouncing off the heavy snowflakes. I remember pulling my sled with a basket full of clothes to be washed and ironed by a woman who helped out when my mom's washing became overwhelming. My uncle, my grandmother, who was old at that time, and my father, and three boys, and my mother, eight people to do all the laundry, plus the cooking, the housework, too much work for one person, and yet she did it without a word of complaint or anger at having the feeling of being put-upon.

I knew it was continuing, her efforts to please and take on too much work for one person, so I became her helper washing dishes, cleaning pans, scrubbing the tile floor, anything to lighten her load. I heard constantly that all this work would kill her. I may have been laughed at as a mama's boy, and I couldn't care less—much of what interested me was outside the caring of others, except for one thing: the movies.

I lived at the Mystic Theatre, the local theatre, it was just three blocks away from our house and you could see a movie for 10 cents and stay as long as you liked. On more than one occasion I would see the same movie two or three times at a sitting, particularly on a Sunday. Weeknights 8 pm was my bedtime, 9 pm on special occasions.

The other interests were the opera on Saturday afternoons and the Toledo Museum of Art, both inspirational outlets for me along with basketball at a place called the Friendly Center.

I love basketball, and I played guard in high school, I really wasn't good enough for first-string, but I was a strong second player. The coach said I had great heart, I was a good guard, but not particularly a good shot—baskets are what count. I was a good backboard retriever, so what? I left the sport. I loved to watch guys out there standing, good enough to be scouted by colleges, and the Harlem Globetrotters, they were really good.

Billy's Case Gets Heard

The mother of the drowned boy insisted his drowning was an act of willful and murderous intent. "The facts are pure and simple," she said. We went to the river and the sand dunes to play, and, you know, walk the rails to see how far you could go without falling off. Tennessee Williams wrote about a play one time called This Property Is Condemned and a young girl is constantly walking the rails. We hadn't read the play, it was something you just do when you live near railroad tracks, it was a balancing act.

We were all walking along the river's edge on the ties that separated the water from the land and the shore, and sometimes the moss on the ties become slimy with water washing over them constantly in hypnotic rhythm. Six or eight kids, I can't remember the exact number, decided to see how far we could all go walking the ties, or the tiles, before we either fell off into the water or we got bored. Billy was the last one on this balancing act, and I can't be sure exactly what happened, but we heard a splash in very quick succession, once, twice, and the third time he didn't come up. None of us were great swimmers, and I believe one of us tried to toss him a belt, and I just remember seeing Billy go down into this muddy river, and the fear was paralyzing, something that just took over.

A life was lost, for some foolish reason, and the next thing I knew I was being slapped across the face to knock me out of this frozen trance, it was a fireman who had been summoned by one of the tugboat men who saw the drowning. Tugboats were always passing, and they must have called the Bridgemen to call the Rescue Squad. After the fireman got me out of this shocked state, I threw up, shaking my body, shaking from the event.

I explained to him what we were doing on the river, playing, just playing as kids do all the time by the river, and even though we weren't supposed to. Our families would be really mad, and of course, a spanking and the usual punishment of being made to stay at home under a watchful eye, tough love is what I'd call it today.

We all went home after the firemen let us go and started to drag the river for Billy. I walked slowly across the railroad tracks, past the boxcars, and up the hill leading to Summit Street, and then home. I dreaded going home for fear of the inevitable.

I entered the house and no one was home. My father was out reading meters and my mother was downtown selling hats, she had not come home just yet. Home, at this time, was the house across from the duplex where we lived with my mother and father after we moved out of the parish house. My other aunt and uncle needed a house to stay in, they had come in from Woonsocket, RI, and they took over for my mother and father. We three boys were getting older and needed more room and a place of our own. The house my mother saw unwanted was across from this duplex, it was for sale, and how we managed to get this house, I am completely unsure of. The one thing I was sure of was her determination to have a home of her own, and she got it with a small down payment and a mortgage.

The house had been beautifully built, it was a shingle type house, home of the owners of the factory down the street, and to this day it's my favorite house. It was to this house that I waited the return of everyone to come into the house.

Somehow they all knew what had happened that day, everything was the opposite of what I had expected. My mother came home first, then my brothers, and then my father. Not much was said, except for their wondering how Billy's mother was, in the tragedy of losing a child.

They were gentle and careful with me, as I was crying half of the time as I told the whole story. We live for an unseen allotted time according to our belief systems and divine providence—they were grateful to God, it was not me, and yet anguished for the mother. The admonition about going down to the railroad was held back until the next day, and it was not long after that that an officer of the law came to the door of our house and asked if I lived there. My mother had answered the door this time, and my brothers had gathered around. I stood there, and once again a sickening fear rolled up in me, as I stood there in my blue shirt and grey-green corduroys and tennis shoes. The officer looked down at me, and he seemed to be ten feet tall.

He informed my mother that I was being subpoenaed for an inquiry into the drowning last week of Billy Gorsuch, also known as Billy. He didn't explain further, and asked my mother and father to please see that I was in court to answer questions about the drowning and the grievances.

I hardly slept for the next week, August; it was in August that we were all assembled into the courtroom. The room was of medium size, dark-wood paneling, benches in the order of pews, and the judge sat high up behind a mahogany desk. There we all were, all six of us who had witnessed Billy's drowning and could do nothing about it, we were truly helpless.

Across the way, the opposite side from us, sat the mother in black, and the one son left her by fates since the husband was killed on his construction site, he was a worker of steel and riveting. We sat waiting for the judge; I couldn't look at her without feeling pain and tears.

The judge came in and we were all motioned to rise, and we sat down after the judge sat. My mind became blank for the first half-hour or so, and then I was startled into reality, and it came crashing down on me.

During the judge's questioning of me it seemed the ordeal had come to the point which the mother could no longer contain herself, and she rose screaming, "Murderers!" If a soul could scream for vengeance, it was here and ever present in this one eruption of volcanic proportions.

Her son was frozen at her side and I sat stunned. The officer of the court came to her side to restrain her and comfort her. The judge asked me to explain the situation to him about that day, and each of us recounted the events as we remembered.

And then, the judge asked me, "Did you in any way push him?"

Through tears and hysteria I explained, "How could I when I was ahead of him?" I went further and told the judge, "I don't know, maybe he hit his head on the ties at the river's edge, I don't know," and I completely broke down.

This was no TV courtroom drama, just as those concerned in this matter. The mother sat in one heap of grief with her son, in a bewildered state.

The judge, at the conclusion of this inquiry, gave his considered verdict, "Not guilty of intended misdemeanor."

If I were to say or write that there was one huge sigh of relief from the accused and their parents, I would be lying. What there was, was a silence, a deafening silence, a frozen silence, you could've cut us out like something out of blocks of ice. The thawing didn't take place until we hit the August sun, the hot August sun.

I had you, oh, for such a short time, so short, and will I ever see you again, hold you again, tell you how much I love you, again? More than anything, so short, so short, so ... short. So much to say has been left unsaid, so much to feel, to tell, so much more to hold, where did it all go?

I can see as I am recounting this memoir, it's taking on a shape, or form, of a mosaic: pieces fitting together as they will in order to form an image. I'm not sure it should continue this way, but at the moment, this is the way it seems to be going.

Childhood

Childhood for me has an extraordinary position in my life; the events of childhood are deeply embedded within me, in my memory, in my body, in my every being.

I remember as a child I would stare out of my bedroom window, waiting for the snow to fall like a man waits for his mistress, it would invariably come long after everyone in the house had gone to bed, and in the stillness of the night, the wind from the outside would whistle past my bedroom window, and the freezing air would paint ice pictures on the windowpane. When the wind died down there would be a time of silence, and then one-by-one the snowflakes would gently fall on the ground below, blanketing the sidewalks and the trees, turning the drab neighborhood into a wonderland of ermine, rich in the whiteness of the fore-frozen rain turned snow.

My heart would creep up my throat and literally convulse into a heartbreaking throb, for no apparent reason, perhaps a forgotten memory of some past time when my soul seemed to remember what lay buried centuries ago. It seemed something so deep, so much apart of me; that the acknowledgment of it would overpower me, drag me back to a time I was just as happy not to recall.

The change of seasons would send my body reeling and shaking as if I had anything to do with this natural phenomenon. Shivering, my body entered each change of season with an erotic shimmer of an orgasm, one gigantic universal seminal explosion that left me exhausted and disoriented, delirious with a kind of happiness that comes only from the discovery of some long, painfully searched for treasure, some elusive dream that materializes just at the point of despair, hardly to be believed in the purity of its execution, seamless in it's perfection: a change had occurred and winter had truly arrived.

I awaited sleep to come and wrap me in her warm, tingling arms. The long awaited-for dreams would invade my body taking me on a journey that imagination would envy. My nerves, jagged and shattered like so many pieces of a mirror splayed into glittering shards reflecting on past and current vignettes of my life, lay scattered like grotesque dolls: a mosaic.

As sleep would wrap me in its care—the day's yelling and shouting from rage because of the seeming futility of some life and whatever broken dreams lay at the edge of the two molding pits of lava that were my parents—had receded into the fog of the day, not forgotten, but seemingly dormant in the cloak of midnight.

My senses remembered it all, and the slightest nod in any direction toward any one of my nerve-ends would bring the events screaming out of me in total recall. The reliving would rack my body like a blistering fever, no way to protect them, not even with my unconditional love of each one, no matter what they did to each other and, sometimes, towards us.

A transparent layer that looked like me and behaved as I did and assumed all of my behavioral patterns began to form as a protective shell. I began to live a life not my own, but one I chose as if it were indeed my own, a surrogate life, one that I had decided to endure, no matter what the consequences were.

Martyrdom took shape early in me; I believed that I could endure pain and suffering much better than anyone else in the world, the true beginning of a martyr's delusion. But, for now, I'm a childhood fantasy who lives in the moment of the time and the season.

CHRISTMAS

Eleven Years Old

It is now winter, the season of Thanksgiving and soon-to-be Christmas; where Mary and Joseph, on an ass, going forth inn to inn looking for a place where the baby Jesus might be born; where the three kings of the Orient would follow the star, leading them to Bethlehem and then the manger; where they would kneel in wonder at the birth of a child who would lay claim to being the son of God and of whom a whole religion would be founded. Practically all the classrooms in the nation would be tuning up their voices preparing to sing the ancient carols—"Joy To The World," "Oh, Come All Ye Faithful," "O Little Town Of Bethlehem," "Away In The Manger," and so many more.

Children would be exhilarated at the thought of being in a play that would enact the hardships of Mary and Joseph's search for a place where the Virgin Mary might bring the Christ-child from the right-hand of God into the world filled with harsh realities of greed and murder, when plots had already been made to kill any child that may have even a hint of fulfilling the prophets' predictions.

But, for the time being, only angels will descend from Heaven singing jubilantly at the birth of the Christ-child and the joy he would bring into the world and the care of all the suffering, all the poor who would feel as if they had finally, finally had someone on their side for a change. One who would defend them from the oppression of the unscrupulous and the murderous rich, from the corrupt officials, and the power-hungry religious leaders of the time. I guess things haven't changed that much anyway.

As a child, the color of Christmas, the glorious music that brings out in celebration of this most miraculous birth, would bring forth in my whole being what Thomas Wolfe refers to as the "squeak" of life, that deep inner-joy of the thrill of just being alive, to having the sensations that make your entire body shiver, as if it were shaking off a cocoon of ice. Christmas was a time of unbridled love, in every direction, no matter what past hurts or grievances had been endured. Whatever racking doubts had crippled my being, a miraculous transformation was in-hand, as stunning as the virgin birth of Christ would overtake me.

I arose the morning after the first snowfall like the phoenix arises from the ashes of its birth. I would feel refreshed and forgiven for all the imagined transgressions I had committed since the beginning of this life, a new start would take place.

Frost Paintings

Part of the reason this transformation took place was prophesied on the window of my bedroom. As the frost began to form its ice pictures, the images they formed revealed to me the events of my life as it was unfolding, and would unfold in the coming days and years ahead. I watched the frost form images of bodies of such staggering beauty, that I knew were as yet to come into being sometime in the future. It nearly drove me out of my mind; scenes resembling wombs or castles, fields of trees and opalescent lakes would take shape on this canvass of glass that we call a window.

On the far right of the window there began to be formed a tree whose shape was at yet indecipherable. Slowly, wisps of feathered branches began to emerge from the bottom up. I couldn't make out what kind of tree it would become, I just had to wait and see what tapestry would reveal to me, the fabric of its life, and when it would look back at its beginning from the very first branch to the very first leaf, it would turn to it's other self and say, "oh, this is what I'm supposed to become."

That is not to say that all is preordained, because I've come to believe that somewhere in the greater cosmos, in the realm of embryonic creation, an agreement was made between God and all living things as to what was needed in the greater scheme of things on this Earth.

Fabric of Our Lives

Somewhere there would be someone or something that needed the complement of another at that particular point in time, much like people know when another person fits, what they have been looking and longing for, to keep them company. You could argue that it seems such a momentary thing, but life is made up of moments strung together that ultimately comprise a life, and the events of that life are made up of moments that are as threads of a tapestry that go to make it up. When they are woven into the warmth of ultimate design, the fabric of our lives, so it was with this frost image forming before my eyes, that cold November night.

I waited silently, my very being anxious at what it would reveal to me. I held my breath to the point where I thought it would knock me out. Slowly, slowly as each branch began to take shape, I would try to guess as to what it would become, as it would reveal itself in its entirety. I can't begin to tell you how long it took, since the time was of no consequence to me. The end of its creation was all, much like my own, mythology, which has since come to drive me around the bend. Nevertheless, I waited at that time because I knew something of personal mythology and behavioral patterns that may have been set a time, a time clock in childhood.

Childhood times, and truthfully, I could still say that I don't understand it, any of it, because it's all guesswork on my part, and that's just fine because I've come to believe that all the experts guess at everything, so why shouldn't I, it's not really important. What's important is what the frost painting would come to be and what it would tell me. Finding the full image presented itself in such a magnificent way, that I lay stunned in frozen form. Here it was, the tree that I'd looked for all of my young life, the tree that I had dreamed about since I had known about it, the one that every child's storybook has pictures of it in such glorious color that it left me breathless every time I looked at it.

The Tree

I couldn't believe my eyes when I saw it there on my window in three-dimensional frost crystals. My God, here was my Christmas tree, thank you Lord, thank you, I just knew it was out there something, and now the only thing that was left was to go out there and find it because I knew it would not have shown itself unless it was ready to be found, and from now on the hunt would begin.

We never, in our house, had had a Christmas tree, as far as I can remember, for no particular reason, other than it was an expense that shouldn't be dealt with at that particular time, as money was scarce, food more important, clothes more important, and a Christmas tree could wait.

Well, I wasn't about to wait; I decided that this time we needed a Christmas tree. I must have been maybe nine or ten and we had to have a Christmas tree, otherwise Santa Claus couldn't come and visit, believe it or not I believed in Santa Claus for the longest possible time.

The backdrop to this window scene was the snow-covered street below, and the sky became filled with crystalline particles that blanketed everything in sight and changed the ordinarily mundane neighborhood into a winter wonderland, the effect was staggering. The trees, the shrubs, everything covered in ice glistened, it was like everything was made of crystal, white crystal, and when the sun happened to hit it, it just let off an incredible kind of aura, and the great elm trees that lined our street were transformed into ice cathedrals, so that the effect of my looking out from my window, with its frost-scene, to the surrounding landscape below, blew my mind. I would go off on a journey of psychedelic proportions that drug-users would've paid a fortune to achieve, and here all it took was to let the imagination run wild.

All I knew or cared about was that the Christmas tree was

coming and with it a cornucopia of longed-for other realities that had little to do with my everyday reality, and much that I had little desire to look at.

All I could think about was that today at five o'clock the radio would bring into our house the voice of Santa Claus for the first time this year, making it official that the Christmas season had begun, that it had arrived. His voice would come roaring out with his "ho ho ho ho ho," and I would literally stick my face in the radio so as not to miss his, "have you been a good boy this year?" and then the carolers would sing out lustily, "you better not shout, you better not cry, you better be good, I'm telling you why, Santa Claus is coming to town." Thank God no one was at home as of yet, because this was a time for me to shed all sense of responsibility to anyone else.

My mother was still at work, my father was asleep upstairs in his room after a hard day of walking all over the city reading water meters, and my brothers were out with their friends doing whatever older brothers do before they're called in to supper. The house is mine for this all too brief and short a time, Santa Claus was all mine. After he signed off I would go outside to shovel the snow off the sidewalk in front of our house, and any of the neighbors I could get to pay me to do theirs for a small fee, just enough time before it got too dark, to be called in to eat supper.

Whatever little I made I gave to my mother, I kept only enough to go to the Mystic Theatre that night, if I could sneak out or find my way out after all the male-Cinderella chores were done, we took turns doing the dishes. God, how I'd wished we had a sister, so she could do the dishes, but all we had was three boys, one of whom was a supreme bully. Suffice to say, I was the youngest, just like Cinderella, only the male version, which should refute all claims made by feminists, that only women suffer the indignities of male oppression. If you're the youngest male in a family of males you'd better rethink that myth, wake up and smell the coffee, as the saying goes, the pecking order of things still exist. Anyway, by hook or crook, I was off to see the movies at The Mystic, and since Christmas was just around the corner, they would be showing something with a Christmastime theme in it.

The Mystic Theatre

Don't get any ideas that The Mystic remotely resembled the fabled movie palaces of yore, this was a neighborhood box, the size of the neighborhood grocery store, filled with popcorn throwing kids rowdy as all hell. Still, it was ours, and it filled many hours of loneliness, it was a place to dream anything that came into your head, and boy, did I do it, I really did.

The movie would invariably be about the perfect mythical screen family laughing up a storm, throwing snowballs on castled-lined streets, whose sweeping, thriving twenty-acre lawns held perfectly formed snowmen and turn around driveways that choke with Packards and Pierce-Arrows of every description and model. The driveways looked like a parking lot for the Fortune 500, and the mother would step out in some smart number by Dior or Madame Boucher to call the children in for tea or cookies and milk, and as they ran in past the ever-mandatory butler, whose name was Jeeves or Goodfellow or some such nonsense.

The camera angle would pan to this huge magnificent tree that took up a good part of this football field size library, and that opened onto this even larger airport that they called a living room. Under this Rockefeller Center size Christmas tree would lay the riches of the Orient, brilliantly wrapped as only the minions of the pharaohs could have conceived to titillate the already over satiated senses of this world weary lord of the then world. Each kid would look like a little Adolf Hitler, what he dreamed of his master race, blonde, blue-eyes, nineteen-feet tall, and a bunch of Brunhildas and Siegfrieds stuffed into the frames of their ten- and eleven-year-old bodies. The manner in which they would tear into these gifts on Christmas morning would strike terror into the heart of "Terminator 2."

Inside these magnificent packages lay brilliantly colored sweaters made of the hairs of soft strands of the chin fuzz of mountain goats from the peak of the Tibetan mountains, which had been woven by blind novitiates of the order of whatever. Then came shoes that had to be cobbled by elves from the North Pole, made of tanned leather of the now extinct herd of unborn unicorns that fed off berries that grew only on the tips of icebergs, wallets stuffed with trust funds that would've been the envy of the owner of Wal-Mart, and next would come sleds designed by NASA, that would fly off into the sky, much like the kids from E.T., yes, E.T., that had become Stephen Spielberg's motion picture and they had been born in place of Louie B. Mayer. Then came dialogue, which went something like this:

"Merry Christmas sweetheart! Did you see what Santa brought you, darling?"

"Yea," came the answer from this giant blue Rhinoceros.

"What's the matter sweetheart, didn't you like what Santa brought you?"

"Yea, they're okay," he answered.

"Tell mommy what you would've liked," then the kid would launch into a list of things that would've made Jackie Onassis blush, if you can imagine that.

(I myself have a hard time wrapping my mind around the prenuptial agreement that she got the Greek zillionaire to sign, not even the rag sheets got a hold of that document. He or she must've been too busy doing whatever in some corner, dreaming up a story about the rape of a celebrity of the instant and soon-to-be-forgotten star of whatever debacle those high-priced, self-styled genius's had signed up, who hold B.A.'s from Harvard and who take intensives from other self-styled genius's about play construction, but who never have sold a fucking outline of a play or a movie, but who are perfectly willing to voice on these elitists the wisdom of the ages as they have gleaned in kindergarten, to show them just how a movie or a play should be constructed and what should happen in the third act. Oops, misspelled happens to the final product, as it has kept the multitudes in droves away from their fifty-million-dollar abortion, now escalated to three hundred million, so much for Harvard B.A.'s and their two day vary intensives from non-performing gurus.)

Meanwhile, back on the screen of The Mystic Theatre, this airs out average—I use the word advisedly—average American family is still engaged in the rape of Christmas morning. Junior has run out into the main hallway that could easily have served as Grand Central Station entrance to the Paris Opera House with its sweeping staircase, ah, home sweet home.

Why is he running out there? Because he had heard Jeeves call out, "Master Siegfried, your father has asked me to usher you to the hall closet," which by the way incidentally serves as the family's hangar for the family airplane that takes them on whatever vacation for this average movie working family, yet I could never figure out what they were vacating from since I never saw them working at anything.

Siegfried comes galloping down the field where Jeeves is about to unveil father's prize gift to his son on this holy morning of Christmas day, Jesus lying, or rather being nailed to the cross. You see, according to the Bible, Jesus has come into this world at this particular time and that the gifts we give to one another are a symbol of those gifts the three kings of the Orient have laid at the feet at the Christ-child, or so I was taught in church, to honor the Lord's gift to the world, a sign of salvation for the human race, Hollywood's version of this event had to be on a grander scale than even the three kings of the Orient could come up with. The "father" in this movie chose to honor his son with gifts as well and, lo and behold, it was his very own fleet, yes, fleet of Rolls Royces to take him to school, one for each day of the year, long before Rodger niece ever came into the scene, they had those Rolls Royces.

"Gee, thanks dad!," came the eloquent spiel from Siegfried's throat, the result of years of tutoring on the people, of people in the movies.

They spoke as if they just gotten off the Queen Mary, "average" Americans that is, according to Hollywood. Then it would be Jeeves' turn to speak, and believe me, this guy had played Hamlet in the West End of London to world acclaim, and he was brought to Hollywood at great expense to appear in this important role of Jeeves, out of these pearls of poetry which gave his family the touch of class they so desperately wanted and needed.

"How doth it please the Master Siegfried, that thy father hath lain before thee these few gifts, in token of his affection toward the goodly self. Thy mother and father wish thee the happiest of Christmas's sire," yes, sire, the most happy of Christmas's, it is apocryphal, but is said that one of the producers came into the writers den shouting, "They didn't say yessiree in those days!" The writer carefully explained to the producer the correct pronunciation of the word "sire," S-I-R-E.

The uncle thought to give the kid a flexible flyer, and with that the kid runs out the door and, Jesus, all I wanted was a Christmas tree. The next shot is the kid running towards the five-acre lawn or twenty-acre lawn poising the sled to hit the ice crust of the snow that meets the sled's runners of steel, taking him on a magic ride of pure joy and ecstasy as I experienced it. I experienced it in my theatre seat watching him with all the vicarious fill that my imagination could muster. After the ride was over I sat, or rather slumped, in my seat exhausted, saying in my head, "please do it again. Please, please, please," but the movie rolled on. As time is money, and if you wanted to experience it again, you'd have to stay and see it all over or come back another night, for which you had to pay another admission fee. They got me over and over again.

In my mind I went over and over the image in my head of

a shot that would be super close to the steel runners, hitting the ice on the sled, cutting into the crusted snow, cutting just deep enough to support the kid on a ride he'd never forget, only this time the kid was me. In my head it was a magic ride, the equal of any that Ali Baba ever took on his magic carpet. It was a ride that Ali Baba had of pure joy, unmixed by any outside consideration or thought of what was possible in the real world. Who could possibly care what any adult would consider the real world, with its stupid idea of limitations.

To Outlast Time

Everything in my mind was busy criss-crossing, just a question of time. The real gamble in life is if you could outlast the time frame of a given said-limit of time that one can set very early in the life of each participant. You being that participant, and the only hitch is that you have to set it early on, otherwise you will have to reprogram that mode as an adult, it can be done, but it's a bitch, and if you want anything, I mean anything, it is possible, just get your ass in gear and move forward, all the stops out.

Every ride thereafter would be a test of my will to recapture the essence of that first ride. Like the first boy's grope towards the sweet breasts of some girl in school that your eyes had followed down the halls every day of your life, every bus ride that took you home riding further than your stop, just to watch her get off first. In spring, my God, it was even more erotic, because she wore layered clothes, which was not to disparage the false sweaters that outlined her young breasts so sweetly. My mind would wrap itself forever around them gently, my God, what a thrill. My mind was busy criss-crossing in all directions with limitless possibilities of sledding and groping at the same time, a veritable feast of erotica. I would play this picture over and over in my mind's eye, the sled ride wearing my insides out, riding at unimaginable speed as my body hurled down the slopes, and then, simultaneously, the imagined sense of the girl's breasts in my hands. I lay exhausted in my theatre seat after the movie was over, too tired to move until the usher would come by to clean up the mess left by half the neighborhood who'd come to see this marathon of Christmas movies.

Roused from this double feature of cinematic excess that really would've rivaled the sacking of Rome, I left the theater hoping not to be screamed at for staying beyond the agreed upon time limit. The walk home in the snow gave me the feeling of what a freefall in space might've been like. A few houses had their lights on and the snow was falling fast and heavy. If you look into one of those glass balls that have the snow scene, shake it, you'll get some idea of how suspended I felt in time on my walk home. The silence was palpable, and so was the thought that hit the pit of my stomach as reality came crashing in. I looked in the modest houses, some of them row houses that lined the walk on the way home.

Home Again

I entered my house by the side door, so as not to track the house full of snow, and I heard on all sides, "Where the hell have you been?" not at all like Jeeves' "Good morning, Master Siegfried," that I had become so quickly accustomed to. So far as I was concerned, the movie kid had it all. I put all that out of my head and thought that Christmas would soon be here in a matter of weeks. I knew it would be of no use, but once my galoshes were off, I would run up the steps from the side door into the living room to see if, by some miracle, there might be a Christmas tree lurking about. No tree, forget it, or as the saying goes "get over it."

The kitchen was warm and the smell of freshly baked bread distracted me long enough to sit through the endless questioning from everyone there, "Where have you been until this late hour?" and one of my brothers would answer, "He was at The Mystic, I'll bet." I said nothing, which of course would drive my middle brother Fred crazy. He never punched me when my mother was around, but he'd save them up for later when he would recite the litany of past transgressions with each blow that he delivered to my arms that were already black and blue from our last punch out.

At that point I didn't care, because the taste of warmly buttered bread had taken over all of my senses and the thought of crawling into bed to see what the "frostman" has left me on my windowpane, or would at least leave me once the outdoor air temperature dropped below zero, would sustain me through any amount of punishment. For some reason the frost pictures were more dramatic the colder it got. Would he leave me my Christmas tree? I could hardly contain myself—the frostman, the frostman leaving me a Christmas tree.

It never became a battle to get me into bed on nights like this, and no one had figured it out. I'm sure they thought that it was to avoid more yelling and looks that said, "Wait, kiddo, until mom's not around." It wasn't dad because he had already been in bed for hours, so it was my mom who kept Fred in check.

My older brother would just laugh at me, or with me, as the case would be. I think Alex liked to see how much I could get away with. More often than not, it was he who took me by the hand and ran me all the way downtown to the real movie palaces. He ran me all the way so that I would be breathless and wouldn't be able to ask him every question in the world. When he did answer, I'd come back with the ever handy "Why?" Being out of breath, I could barely talk, which was just fine with him.

He was extremely generous to me, and loving, and when there was time, he'd buy me hotdogs at this great hotdog stand, and popcorn for the movies when we got there; he was the ideal big brother. I guess God, in his infinite wisdom, figured he should balance things out, he should've done the same for Cinderella.

Once in bed I'd fall asleep to wait for my dream, the frost-man did even better this night, for he slowly created the bodies of a couple in love, an embrace that I would now identify as a loving couple that Rodin had created in marble.

The slow revelation of this erotic couple was no match for my imagination that had them in every conceivable position doing God knows what, and I almost forgot about my Christmas tree, but the insistent thought of no Christmas tree gave me no peace. Where was my Christmas tree?

Slowly off to the side, it formed a larger Christmas tree than ever. The hot, moist air from the kitchen floated up and steamed the entire house and all the windows made it easier for the frostman to go crazy, and he did, a real Michelangelo of ice and frost. "If it's on my window, why isn't it in this house," I reasoned. "Christmas is coming, does anyone around here know that? Christmas isn't Christmas without a Christmas tree." I could no longer resist sleep, and I lay dreaming of my tree. Night after night the same ritual took place on my windowpane, sometimes the pictures would change, but always my tree would appear somewhere on the landscape of frost.

Santa's Voice

Five o'clock in the afternoon was the magic hour, when Santa's voice would come through the radio speaker, and always I prayed that the house would be quiet. I rushed into the house from the side door pulling off my galoshes as fast as I could. Throwing off my canvas bag that I carried my newspapers in, left over from my paper route, it was never more than one or two, due to the fact that someone moved out without paying me, and I could get stuck for the week if I didn't report it to the road manager. But never mind that, for the time being I had to hear Santa no matter what. As I raced for the radio to catch Santa's "ho, ho, ho" and the inevitable, "have you been a good little boy or girl? You better be, because I'll be coming to your house with presents if you have, and if you haven't, you'll be very sorry. So, you better not shout, you better not cry, you better be good, I'm telling you why, Santa Claus is coming to town."

I would shout into the radio, "Wait! We don't have a tree yet! And I know you didn't come last year because we didn't have a tree for you, but this year I promise you we will!" Somehow I thought Santa could hear me, "I promise you we will. Well, I know we never had one before, but this year we will, we will. And listen, I won't ask for anything else, I promise you. You can ask God if I haven't been a good boy. I give all the money from my paper route to my family, to my mother really, who buys the groceries for all of us. So, with what little that amount of money could buy, I did buy the groceries for all of us," or so I thought, "so with what my father gives her money for groceries, and what I give, we can buy a little more, and then when it snows I get money for shoveling sidewalks. So you see how good a boy I've been? All I want is a tree as beautiful and green, like the ones they have in the Christmas books, and I'll just love it, I'll really love it always, I will, and I won't ever ask for anything ever again. Just this once, please, please, please. Oh, and I'm an altar-boy in church, and you can ask God if you don't believe me, and my uncle is an archbishop in the Orthodox Church, he heads all of the diocese's of America, North America and Canada and Mexico. Of course, I'd get killed if I didn't go to church, being the archbishop's nephew."

"I'm awfully tired of being an example; it's just too hard. But I do it just the same because they all really wanted me to be a priest and follow in his footsteps, but I have to be honest with you, I don't want to be a priest, it's too hard, and I don't think I'd like God watching everything I do. It's bad enough that I feel guilty if I play with myself past midnight on Saturday, because it's really Sunday, God's holy day, and I don't think he'd like it if he thought I was being disrespectful on his day, or any day. As far as I could make out, there's a no-no at any time. I'm only eleven and it's gonna be too long before I get married, that's a long way off, and what am I gonna do with all these feelings until then? I promise I won't touch myself until the Christmas tree comes, and then I'll even try to hold out longer if I can, just to have my tree. And Santa, it doesn't have to be like the one in the movies, it can be any kind of tree, bare on one side, I can put that up against the wall so no one will even see it, it'll be just fine. Only, please, please, please hurry." I talked to him as if he were there in the room with me, and so with one ear I'd listen to Santa while I talked to him before he got away.

I had to get in as much as I could before he started his "ho, ho, ho! I've gotta go now boys and girls, so remember, be good and when you're fast asleep I'll be coming to your house on Christmas Eve. On Prancer, on Dancer, on Blitzen," on, on, on, etcetera, I can't remember all of them. And then, the sound of bells jingling and the swish of the sled going off in the distance, with Santa's laughing voice becoming more faint by the second. No painting by Norman Rockwell or N.C. Wyeth could match the images conjured up in my imagination, and when Santa came into my life every afternoon at 5 pm, nothing seemed to be able to compete with the fantastic world I inhabited, and it's been a bitch trying to figure out why they don't match more often.

The Child Within Us

I suspect that as adults we're made to feel ashamed of that child within each of us, the child that never really dies, but gets shoved off into a corner because it doesn't seem to fit in the real world, especially as an adult, whatever that is. Snow covers a lot of the ugliness, and do you suppose it's the same in the landscape of the mind? I really wonder. Christmas Eve is coming up, and soon, and still no tree. "Ho, ho, ho," five o'clock, Santa's voice, all the insistent signals of Christmas Day.

I looked out the window, the snow was falling, the house was still, and no one was around. I thought to myself, "Where is everyone?" I looked all over for signs that someone knew what day it was. Where's the tree? I was going nuts. Outside the snow is falling harder; I sat quietly waiting to see if anyone would show up. Maybe they were out buying presents, fat chance, but still, I could hope, couldn't I? The ringing of the phone startled me, and I ran to pick it up.

"Hello, hello," came this voice from the other end,

And I answered, "Hi, mom."

"Hi sweetheart," she said, "I'm gonna be a little late. I'm gonna be working late tonight at the store. The store is filled with ladies buying hats, and they are trying on everything in the store. Mrs. Fields has asked me to stay longer to help her out. So, heat what's in the oven and I'll be there before we go to church," and I heard her say to someone, "I'll be right there. Be a good boy sweetheart," and the phone hung up with a click.

My mother worked in a ladies' hat store, and I remember the few times I visited her there. On a couple of occasions, Mrs. Fields hired me at slave wages to put away all these goofy looking hats. I watched the salesladies lying through their teeth about how smart one customer looked in that abortion called a hat, and how it picked up the color in her eyes, and how chic it was on her, a French word that added a touch of class to this maison de chapeaux, French for hats, pure sales bullshit. No wonder the saleslady would call out, "uh, Mrs. David, this patron is asking for you. Mrs. So-and-so would like to see you when you're finished with other Mrs. So-and-so. Would you care for Mrs. Uplift? Would you care for her?"

All these ladies must've seen the same movie because that's the way all the salesladies talked, like Carole Lombard in her latest movie when she went shopping for a hat, the trickle down theory of manners and behavior according to Hollywood.

I was hungry, so I looked in the oven and there was a tray of already cooked string beans with lamb and a separate pot of rice. I hated string beans at that time, and lamb, and I told my mother a thousand times how I hated it. She makes them anyway because my brothers like them and so does my father—well, what about me? I should've gotten that message a lot earlier than I did, and for that matter, the whole message of life: if you want something, go get it for yourself, and never mind the past sacrifices you've made, because in essence, you did them for yourself.

For any number of reasons that Freud or Carl Gustav Jung may have been able to enlighten you on, I didn't think about the cost because it would be cheaper in the end. Please believe me, because I do know that for sure.

Back to the beans and no tree. My dad is from the old country, and he wouldn't spend a nickel for a tree, and my mother was too busy being innovative about how to make potatoes ninety-thousand ways to Sunday, with ring bologna and other culinary delights. But in fairness to her, she did better than most would have, and besides, she baked the greatest apple pie this side of heaven. You couldn't add to that, her being run ragged trying to make fat, ugly ladies look like Carole

Lombard or Joan Crawford in hats that would look better on lamps or small birds. With this sense of urgency, and the deadline of Christmas at hand, I ran up the stairs to the bed where I slept and pulled the mattress aside revealing the exposed bed-coils in the springs that held two one-dollar bills.

I was going to buy a Christmas present for everybody at the drug store with money that I kept from my paper route, just for this purpose, but I decided that since no one was going to buy the tree, the house would get the tree as a gift from me, and that was just too bad for them. I was gonna have a tree, come hell or high water, because Santa Claus had to have a tree so that he could leave me a gift when he passed over our house, this Christmas I was not going to be left out.

You see, I'd had a paper route that my elder brother Alex had convinced the paper route manager that I could handle. It started with twenty-four customers, in and around our neighborhood, the first year, and it grew little by little each year, as I got older. In past years, some people skipped out on me, so by this time, I'd wised up and I made all of them pay for their papers a week in advance. You heard me, a week in advance. That way it wouldn't be too much on them, and I'd be able to pay my route bill on time with no loss of money to me, and no skip-outs.

That year, I acquired the tugboat house down by the river, and I didn't tell my family because the banks of the river are treacherous and it had already cost a few families their kids. I took it because I had heard that when it came Christmastime they gave the paperboy a dollar as a bonus, and I wanted that dollar. Listen, a dollar at that time was a lot of money, and now it came in handy. This little bit I perceived as greed, on my part, for not giving up every last cent I had to my mother, to supplement my father's income; more truthfully, in hopes that it would cut down on the fights over money.

A Two-Dollar Tree

Something that plays over and over in my memory, to this day, since I didn't care for dinner or what had been prepared, I thought it more important to start on my quest for a two-dollar tree. I grabbed my winter mackinaw, pulled on my wool-stocking cap, ran down the stairs, shoved on my galoshes, and ran out the side door into what was starting to be a blizzard. This Christmas Eve was going to be picture beautiful, just like Dickens wrote about in his stories. Don't ask me why, but the thought of England just made me cry, and this Christmas Eve there was going to be a tree in this house, come hell or high water.

I walked along Summit Street, which is the street parallel to our street, Superior Street, because it ran parallel to the river. I remember seeing a couple lots where they sold trees, I couldn't remember exactly where they were, and in this snowstorm everything looked a little different. I'd been on the bus on my way to Boys Club to play ping-pong when I spotted these tree lots. The Boys Club was formed by a lot of old guys who'd made it in life and built it as a testament to their humble beginnings. I was still both, that is, beginning and, God knows, humble.

I really hated the idea of humble, and without all the money I thought necessary to ease the pain of arguments and yelling, but more so after seeing so many movies where everyone in it rode around in long black limousines a half a block long, with chauffeur-driven cars, opening the doors for everybody. They seem to be protected from all the ugliness of the world around them, much like the emergence of a butterfly from its cocoon.

I thought, if an ugly worm, in its beginning, can turn into a magnificent butterfly, so can I. My mind flipped into a world of crystal and diamonds, and Persian rugs knee deep in famous people, but I'll think about that later, right now the snow was hitting my face, blinding my vision, and I had to find this lot with my tree. As it got colder, as the wind whipped off the river, my hands got numb from the freezing wind, and from a distance I could see a string of light bulbs. I hoped that it would be the lot where my Christmas tree was.

As I got closer I saw this man huddling around an open fire, stamping his feet to stay warm. I tried to approach the lot as nonchalantly as possible, so as not to look as desperate as I felt inside, and believe me, I was one desperate kid on this Christmas Eve. My heart leapt at the sight of all the trees. Was my Christmas tree here? It had to be, it just had to be.

My eyes quickly searched the entire lot, like an eagle searching for its prey. I walked around, and then into the heart of the lot, I thought I saw one that may be my tree, I couldn't tell, because the snow almost covered it completely from sight. In a voice that trembled from fear and anxiety, I heard my voice croak out, "How much is that tree over there, sir?" I thought that the "sir" was a good way to start off because it might ease the pain of what I feared would be this answer,

"That one?"

"Yes sir, that one."

"Well kid, you got a good eye," and with that answer, I knew I was in trouble, you don't have to be old to experience a sense of vibration of things, and his voice carried the vibration that rattled my inside like a boxer's punch to the stomach, "Son, that there tree is a true Northern Balsam from Northern Canada"—the word northern twice in the same sentence made it seem like it came from Santa's own Christmas tree lot on the North Pole, God, was I in trouble, and I hadn't even begun the search.

"How much is it, please," my voice squeaked out.

"I'm afraid that there tree there is more than you've got, son." When anybody calls you "son," it should be a danger signal; as far as I'm concerned, and this was no exception.

Again, I said, "How much is it, sir?" I kept on.

"Twenty dollars, son." I thought that the Earth would open up and swallow me whole.

"But it's Christmas Eve, and no one's around now," I kept up, in spite of my feelings.

"You don't know much about human behavior, son," there went that "son" again.

"I do, because I'm a paperboy."

"Well, that's good, son. But I'll bet it takes you a long time to earn that kind of money on a paper route."

"Yes, sir, it does, but right now no one is around, and it's Christmas Eve."

"That's when a lot of people come out to buy a tree," he said.

"Do they?" I asked.

"Well, you're here, aren't you?"

"Yes, but I'm the only one. I'm the only one in my house who seems to care about having a tree."

"You Jewish?" he said.

"What's that?" I answered.

"C'mon kid, you mean you don't know what a Jew is?" He looked kind of funny at me, and I took note that this was the first time he called me "kid."

I didn't know about words as well as I would grow to learn their value, but somehow I understood the vibration of that word, and I was fully aware of that particular vibration. From the very first sung, something hovered over me, a sensation that I didn't like, and it made me feel strange, but I ignored it because what I had in mind was one thing, and that was my tree.

"All I know is people are people, and some are good, and some aren't so good."

"I can see you've got a lot to learn," he said. He looked at me and something in his eyes took on a hard, cold stare, it was as if he were making up his mind about something, a game plan or something. "Let me give you a lesson, kid, in human behavior. People wait 'til the last minute to do things, and tonight a wife will get on some guy's back to go out and buy a tree, and she don't care what he has to pay for it, as long as there's a tree for junior to wake up in the morning so he could see it. C'mon back here to the rear of the lot and I'll show you a beauty of a tree, that's just waiting for some sucker who waited 'til the last minute to buy a tree."

I got an even funnier feeling in the pit of my stomach, but my desire to see what I thought just might be a match to the frostman's tree on my windowpane outweighed the strange sensation crawling over my skin.

He turned and started to slowly walk to the rear of the lot saying over his shoulder, "C'mon kid, follow me a little ways over here."

"You keep the beautiful big ones back there?" I blurted out.

"Yea, just a little ways back here," his voice trailed off, "C'mon, I'll show you."

God, why does everyone hide things where a kid can't find them? Why aren't they out in the open? A lot should be out in the open, I thought to myself. I slowly trudged my way in the deep snow towards the back of the lot, further and further from the street than I would've liked. He stopped at the overturned tree that looked like a huge fat log; he stood waiting for me to come closer. I reached the spot where he was standing, and his tall body looked like the Green Giant, only his face wasn't jolly. I arrived a little out of breath, and I could feel the steam pouring out of my mouth, wrapping itself around my face; as I moved in with each trudging step, my face felt moist with it.

The snow was falling harder, so that there seemed to be a veil of snow covering the distance between us, like two figures upright in a glass ball. There was a moment's hesitation before he spoke, "You wanna see how big this tree is?" he said in a way that carried more than what the words were supposed to mean. There was a seemingly avuncular, unctuous quality to his voice that oozed more than sounded.

Jesus, I was scared shitless, and didn't really know what this guy had in mind, but I looked around and thought, if I had to run, there was no clear path for me to sprint, I'd have to take three steps to his one bounding leap. I began to feel like a trapped animal. He reached into his coat pocket and brought out a switchblade that seemed to crack as it cut the freezing night air. The blade caught the light of the dim overhead bulb, and gleamed with a dirty haze, as if it had old encrustations of blood, not wiped clean from its last episode.

My body became wet instantly, and a warm trickle of water streamed down my leg. I'm peeing, I thought, I'm peeing my pants! My God, all I want is a Christmas tree, and this is what's happening to me?

He took the knife and started to bend over the log to begin cutting the trees that bound it, or so I thought. He looked over at me from his crouched position, and he became a black bear in my eyes, his face was red, and he smiled at me. His teeth looked like fangs, and my voice caught in my throat and strangled any sound that might've come out.

Spit ran down the side of his mouth, he hadn't made a move, but a crack caught inside me and started to split my insides wide open. I prayed I would instantly become nineteen feet tall with hands that contained razors, and feet that automatically grew spikes the size of drills pointed to the sharpness of Damascus steel blades.

I would be ready to turn to him in a state of blood, pus, and mucus, easy to mix with the snow as raspberry sherbet gone rotten. I tried to keep from throwing up, and barely managed to do so, when a man's voice called out, "Hello! Hello! Anybody here?"

Tense moments lapsed before this shit-kicking voice

came out of this guy, dripping with the thickness of black-strap molasses, "Yea, I'm back here with this kid, showing him what a Christmas tree oughtta look like."

I could barely pick my feet up from the exhaustion of what seemed to be a near-battle for my life for whatever this asshole may have had in mind, and I'm sure he had something, and it wasn't a tree. I couldn't talk for the longest time, and as he walked towards me, he laid his paw on my shoulder, and just as quickly I knocked it off with a violence that startled even me.

I wasn't sure whether this man caught this move or not, but I wasn't hanging around to find out, my little body bounded out of the snow and trenched the lot like a jackrabbit.

"Don't you wanna see this here big tree, son?" his voice called out after me as I heard him laugh out loud.

I heard him say to the man that "This tree came from way up north and blah, blah, blah, blah." I ran as if my life depended on it, and somewhere inside me I knew that it did, or at the very least an experience I would not have liked.

I ran with all my heart until I felt sure I was well out of the area.

I ran through alleys that I knew would let me out onto the street far away from this lot. I passed another lot where a couple and their kids were shopping for a tree too. It seemed like that asshole was right after all; people do shop for trees at the last minute. When I grow up I'm going to shop for my tree right after Thanksgiving and not wait 'til the last minute.

I watched them shake every tree in the lot; it looked as if they were murdering them.

The man's voice rang out, "What do you think of this one, hun?",

The woman's voice rang out in a return yodel, "See if you can't find one a little smaller. That one might be too hard to trim, hun."

The lot owner shot back, "I'll show you a beaut, but it'll cost you, because it's a Balsam. C'mon over here and see this one, and bring the little wife," that was a huge compliment, because as far as I could see, she dwarfed her husband and son in girth, and I could see that junior took after her, as far as size goes, and I watched him attack each tree like it was a personal enemy, God help the tree when he finished with it. I watched all this from a distance, while trying to collect myself, after the last ordeal, and to try to regain my courage to approach any tree lot owner from here on in. I didn't feel like this was my lot and it was growing late.

I heard the woman say, "That's too much money to spend on a tree when we're going to throw it out in a couple of days, hun."

I slowly trudged away from the lot, and it was snowing harder than ever now. "Oh God, would I ever find a tree for two dollars," I thought.

I heard the owner say, "Ma'am, you're not going to find a prettier tree anywhere, and especially a Balsam this size. It's getting late, and I saved this one for me, but I'll give it to you because it's Christmas Eve and I'm getting ready to close pretty soon."

I had no idea how late it was, but I thought, "I can't go home without a tree," and besides, my insides were tightened enough to give me a stomach ache. Why do things always have to come down to the last minute with me? I hated the patterns of my life, so far, and it seemed as if I let others dictate the events of my life. I should've said, "the hell with it," and gone out and bought the tree as soon as I had the two dollars, and not worried about presents for everyone, but of course, I didn't, because I wanted them all to know how much I love them, and I felt that I'm the one that should try to make them happy. I know, wrong, but, that was me, and still may be me for all of my experience and self-awareness of the world and the order of things that go to make up this journey we call life.

I started to feel so frustrated, that I, for some unknown reason, just began to cry softly. Not so much cry, as a silent welling-up of my eyes, the tears fell down my cheeks and would have frozen had my body not gushed forth heat from rage, anger, and a sense of futility. I prayed silently for guidance and mercy on this "orphan in the storm," that's what I thought of myself as, an "orphan in the storm."

Deals with God

I made all kinds of deals with God, vowing all sorts of things, if only it would help me find a tree, after all, it didn't seem like such a selfish act, it seemed only fair that I who had worked for most things that I got, should at least have a tree to celebrate his birth. So, you see, it was for him, as well as for me, and the fact was that I needed a tree for Santa to come to my house to give me a present was incidental, in my child mind, one which I may still have to this day, not may, I'm almost totally sure I still think that way at times, but I'm improving, and still working on it. Does that come under the lessons learned, or needed to learn, on this journey called life?

I walked in a daze, not sure where I was going. I decided to walk back to the tree lot to see how things were progressing with this all-American family; after all, the whole family unit was there, the kid wasn't out all alone. God, I hate self-pity, but I'm afraid I was indulging in it rather heavily, like an "orphan in the storm."

As I got closer, I could hear the owner's voice selling these people on this tree, "Perfect, isn't it?" he said, and it was, it was beautiful. I could see from where I stood that the branches were thick and dips into the light that hung overhead, there was just enough separation between each branch to hang ornaments and icicles.

He grabbed the branch between the palm of his hand and proffered his palm for them to smell, "Here," he said, "you can smell all of Northern Canada right here in the palm of my hand, and when you get this indoors it'll make your whole house smell of the fresh scent of pine." Believe me, I could smell it already as he talked, and it was as clean a smell as you could wish for, just wonderful. I watched as the wife came over with the kid in tow, talk about conflict, my mind was racing with all sorts of thoughts, not all of them Christian. I saw them

126

all swallowed up whole, with the tree standing on the edge of the abyss, waiting for me to come and rescue it from the fires of hell, a good deed in my eyes. After all, I couldn't save the poor people, because they'd already disappeared in this huge crater, but the tree was standing right there, waiting for me to rescue it from a certain destruction, a loss in anybody's books to the spirit of Christmas, and I would be it's savior.

I came to when I heard the woman say, "Oh, alright, if you want to pay that much for it, but don't let me hear you say you're broke the next time we go shopping."

"Tie her to the car, you made the sale," said the husband.

The kid let out a scream that curdled my blood, "It'll be beautiful in our house dad! Thank you, thank you, thank you!"

A stillness covered my body and my mind, for whatever reason, I was numb, but in the silence of night there seemed to be a crack, a sharp crack, like lightning splitting the atmosphere breaking the perfect symmetry of the snow flakes that fell around me, and when I looked at the ground, rather than star-shaped flakes, there were these broken crystals at my feet.

Is it possible that the disturbed energy that surrounds a person also disturbed the planes of atmosphere surrounding that person? I felt an anger rise up in me that disturbed the very snow that fell in my vicinity, and spoiled what was perfection in nature, much the same as individuals who are heavy with rage and despair, difficult to be around, and make it virtually impossible to be in their company.

A voice came at me from behind that shook me out of my seemingly altered state, " I'll tell ya, they always leave things 'til the last minute, believe me, I know people alright," he said laughing to himself as he carried the tree to the waiting car.

All I could think of was, "You just wait, I'll find a bigger and a better tree. You just wait and see if I don't."

The wind got increasingly colder as the night wore on, and coming off the river, it made it even colder, freezing is a better word. My nose began to run, and the mucus crystallized on the lining of my nasal passages so much so that I began to feel as if someone had packed my nose with ice. It was getting darker and time seemed to be passing by very quickly. The spell of Christmas Eve wore down on me, and made me more anxious with each passing second. The snow had piled high everywhere, and everywhere you looked there were huge banks of it.

I came upon a rather forlorn-looking lot that had a few trees, and what there were looked barren and scraggly. I wondered, "Why cut the poor things down? No one's gonna want them, so why cut them?" I tried to picture what it would be like at home. There would be a lot of yelling and shouting and, most likely, a whack at my behind for being out after dark. I don't care, because once they see this beautiful tree I'm gonna bring back, they might not. The scenario played over and over in my head. When I had awakened from this reverie, I seemed to be lost in an area I had never known, or had never seen before. Could this possibly be? Well, I was an explorer, and the number one thing on my mind was that I wanted a tree. I had walked the area around my neighborhood until I knew every tree and bush in the summer, and especially those that bore fruit, since I always availed myself to them when they were ripe, and not always with the owner's permission.

Things looked strange to me now, what with the wind whipping everything up in the snow flurries, made things look like those balls of glass filled with water that held a snowman, and when you shook it, it made like a winter storm effect. The hour's getting late, but somehow time had seemed to stop. I'd put my head down into the wind as the snow started to turn into crystals of ice that I knew had come in off the wind of Lake Erie.

I Seemed to Be Lost

When I picked up my head, I seemed to be lost, everything had a deathly quiet cast to it, and I no longer recognized anything. I tried to find the river that I knew was but a block away from my house, but there didn't seem to be a river anywhere, not anywhere in sight. I cut through an alley that I thought I remembered, where there was a Michigan cherry tree, that every time I passed, all I could think of were those cherries in the form of a wonderful pie, there was nothing like that kind of pie, juicy and a sweet and sour taste that lingered in your mouth like a dream remembered. One thought flashed quickly in my mind, only six months to go for cherry season.

As I came out of the alley I saw in the distance a string of lights that had to herald the presence of a lot, I could barely make it out, what with the snow coming down in sheets now, and the closer I got I kept repeating to myself, "It has to be my Christmas tree lot," over and over like a mantra of sorts. A short distance away, I could see what looked like a bonfire with an old man standing in front of it, keeping warm I suppose.

"I don't remember this lot at all," I whispered aloud to myself. I had a habit of talking to myself more often than I would like, and it gets me into trouble. "Did it just spring up out of nowhere?" I asked myself, "I don't remember this lot at all."

I walked faster and then broke into a run, I was really so excited, screaming into the night, "Hey, hey! Are you open? Please, please be open!" My warm breath filled the night air like a cloud of white smoke, I nearly ran into the man, "Have you got any trees left?" I shouted at the man. I was so out of breath I nearly fell on my face.

"What are you blind? Look around, see for yourself, I got plenty left," he said.

As I looked around the lot there was only one tree standing in the center of the lot, and I looked at the man standing in front of the fire, and he was wearing a cap that had earmuffs attached to it, a long, flowing scarf of every color in the rainbow, and a large three-quarter mackinaw jacket, black wool pants, and shiny black winter galoshes with white lamb's wool cuffs at the top. I looked at him, not quite sure about his state of mind. One tree in the lot, and he says, "I've got plenty."

"I see only one," I said to him.

"Are you gonna need more than one?" he said.

"No, but I-I, I stammered.

"No buts, just go and look at her," this is what he said to me.

"Well, I don't know, the lots I've seen had a whole bunch to look at," I replied rather sheepishly.

He looked at me for a long time, and I heard him say, "What do you need a whole bunch for when you have one perfect one right here, to choose from."

I stood, lost in a daze, "If you have a choice, you can pick a good one that might not cost as much, and I know that that tree is gonna cost a lot of money, because it is the most beautiful tree I have ever seen," I said.

"How do you know so much?" he said.

"Because I've been all over looking for the tree, all the trees," I said, "and I've seen there aren't nearly half as beautiful as this, cost twenty-thirty dollars," so I figured this tree had to be a lot more.

Some time passed as he stood there watching me, and then he finally spoke up, "Aren't you gonna go over and look at it?"

I just stood there without answering him, because, really, I could hardly talk, and that's unusual for me. I can't be sure just what was going on inside my little body, I started to shake and shiver, my voice was trying to form some kind of sentence, but nothing would come out of my mouth, very unusual for this talkative youngster. He said nothing, but continued to stare at me. It seemed as if my throat had frozen in the freezing night air, I was a mass of unidentified emotions. I felt the gentle shove of his hand pushing me in the direction of that solitary tree standing majestically in the center of this lot. I moved toward it, rather in slow motion, time had stopped and the atmosphere was without a sound of any kind, I was alone in the world, in space being directed by an energy that had no reference, no reference to anything in my life at this point.

I could only guess that it came from him, this stranger that looked so ordinary, a grandfather figure with a kind face. As I approached the tree I stretched my hand out, removed my mittens, and closed the palm of my hand around the lower branch and pulled it gently toward me feeling the soft pine needles brush my inner palm with the faintest sensation of silk and oil coating the skin. I raised my palm to my nostrils and the richest odor of fragrant Balsam Pine, the only one that smells like that, shot through my nasal passages to the back of my head, exploding like so many starburst fireworks on the fourth of July, I was dizzy with the sensations of the universe in one bolt of awareness of the power of nature, it was magical.

A squeak of joy hit my stomach, a bubble of laughter rose from my throat thawing the frozen ice that lay blocking the sound that was hidden behind this glacier, and it was forth in a cascade of thrilling giggles, high pitched laughter and a flood of tears, "it's a Balsam! It's a Balsam!" I shouted, "it's a Balsam!"

The old man smiled at me and said, "I see you know your trees, alright."

"No, but I remember the smell from another tree, and it was a Balsam, because a man, at the other lot, showed me how to tell a Balsam from other kinds, and it's so different,"

I answered, "that I could never forget that smell." I looked at him more closely, as he was standing but a few feet away from me, he was framed backlit by the street lights, the snow falling all around him, his face had little about it that would distinguish him from any other old man that you had seen before, and yet, there was something odd about him, something gentle and touching. The overriding thought was, "Boy, how much would this tree cost, since it was twice as large as the other trees that I had seen and more than I could ever afford, at least at this time."

My face must have shown this horrific thought, because I heard him say, "What's the matter?" Well, I wasn't sure how to begin without sounding as if I was begging, and yet, I desperately wanted this tree. "C'mon son, tell me what's on your mind?"

I looked at the tree, and then at him, and somehow I knew that he was waiting for me to use my own language, and my own expression of what it was that I wanted. Words rarely failed me and, very often, they were bullshit packaged in a razzle-dazzle manner, in a kind of artful dodger way that had balls, but lack real substance. I had grown accustomed to lying, faking to the left to obtain what I wanted, and somehow, I got a lot, but ultimately I would only learn later on in life that was too high a price, part of my soul and integrity leading to a loss of self-respect and self-esteem would ultimately be the price.

I lived for the moment only, and at this very instant none of that came out, only the real of me, the real me, evidence itself, and I was at a complete loss. I knew instinctively that only the truth, right now, would pass muster.

"I don't have anywhere near the money this tree is worth," and with that I walked slowly away from the tree of my life, the gift I had thought was for others, I now knew was for me, and me only, I had much to learn.

I saw him look at me with an impassive face, just looking

at me as I moved on by him when I heard his voice say, "Are you sure?" I didn't know how to answer him.

So, I just shook my head, not in any hangdog fashion, I knew I'd come up against something that I wasn't sure what it was, and I seemed to be at peace for the first time in a long time in my very young life. It was almost as if I didn't need it anymore, I've rarely had that feeling since, but I think I now know what it is.

"Wait a minute," he said, "Do you want this tree, or don't you?"

I faced him and said in a voice I had never heard myself use before, "That's alright. I only wanted it for me."

"What's wrong with that?" he said.

"I thought I wanted it for my brothers, and my father, and my mother, but I really only wanted it to please myself," that's what I had answered.

Again came, "What's wrong with that?"

"Well, you're not supposed to be selfish and want things only for yourself."

He answered, "Who says?"

"It's in the bible."

"Where?"

"I don't know, but I know it's in there somewhere."

"Show me."

"I don't have a bible on me, but it's in there somewhere. Don't you believe me?"

"Oh, I believe that you believe that it's so, but I'm here to tell you that it's not true."

I just stood there, wanting to believe that, but somehow I couldn't. "Did you ever hear of sharing?" he said.

"Of course, it's what I've tried to do all my life. I mean, I give most of my money from my paper route to my mother for groceries," I said.

"Well, that's nice. But, what do you give all the others in the house?"

"What do you mean?"

"Just what I said, what do you give all the others in the house?"

Well I stopped for a moment, "Well, I uh-um-uh-I don't have anything left, and besides, it's for everybody."

"What was that?" I was beginning to get flustered and kind of sore at this guy for asking all these questions.

"I said I don't have anything left!" I shouted.

"Oh, well, you don't have anything left? Well, now, who's fault is that?" I stood there shocked because I wasn't sure what this guy was getting at, but I wanted to cry for no apparent reason that I could understand. I felt helpless and confused, and I knew he was trying to tell me something, but what it was I couldn't really get to.

He studied me for a long time, and then he gently began to explain to me the sophistication of this complex philosophy in very simple terms, at least simple terms that I could understand, "If you have a nice-sized apple and you give it only to one person, only that person gets to eat the apple."

"But, sir, the food is for all of us," I interjected.

"That's true. But what do you have left to give when you've given it all away, and there is an urgent need for some of it now?"

I thought for a moment, "I'll ask God for it."

"Well, that's a good answer, but suppose he's busy with the others who may need it more than you at this very moment that you need it."

"I really don't know how to answer that," so I said, "Look, I'm only eleven."

"Well," he said, "Then act like eleven."

"But aren't you supposed to help your family all that you can?"

"Sure," he said, "you're supposed to help them all that you can, but even in nature, fruit trees don't give fruit before their time, not until they're mature, and then they give for the rest of their life, because at that time of their bearing of fruit, they give all their fruit to the owner, who shares it with his or her family and friends. But the strength of the tree, the sap, the blood in the veins of that tree isn't given away because it needs it to make more fruit next year and all the years to come."

Well, I didn't really understand all this, but I couldn't begin to have this kind of discussion with him, it seemed rather foreign to me, this thinking of his, he was a nice man, and I didn't want to hurt his feelings. The strange thing was that I forgot the freezing cold for the time being, because I was so busy trying to figure all of this out. It was true, I only had two dollars on me for a tree that I thought was the most beautiful Christmas tree I had every seen.

"How much money do you have on you for a Christmas tree?" he said.

Sheepishly, I answered, "two dollars."

He said, "What?"

"Two dollars," I mumbled. "Two dollars," I said a little louder.

"Well, are you ashamed of it?"

"No, I earned it on my paper route."

"Well then speak up, you act like you're ashamed of it. You didn't steal it from anybody, and it's yours. So, be proud of it and stop mumbling."

"I worked for it!," I shouted at him, "And I got a dollar from the tugboat house because it's a dangerous customer down by the river, where a lot of kids have drowned. So, they give a paperboy a dollar at Christmastime, because they know that a lot of boys won't deliver it to them, but I wanted that dollar so much, so I just did it. And nobody knows but me and the paper route manager, and it's really not that dangerous if you just deliver it and get out of there," I said it in a breathless and hurt fashion as if the faster I said it, the sooner I would imaginatively get away from this river that drowned so many of my friends.

"Well, you want that tree, or don't you?" He started bearing down on me to speak up and say what it was what I wanted. It seemed that when I wanted something of importance, really important to me, I became unable to ask for it, for fear of rejection. So, I would hedge or couch the request in such a way that my true meaning was blurred, unclear in every respect, so as to confuse the granter, or would be granter, and leave them in an altogether bewildered state, "What does he want" attitude, and rather anxious to get the ordeal over with, and more likely than not, reply in the negative, or just plain "no."

I was in such a mode at this moment, and he knew it, but he was so patient with me, that I was dumbfounded. I was really dumbfounded at not being brushed aside and made to feel unimportant, as kids are often made to feel, and this kid in particular. I armed myself early and said in a rather soft voice, "Yes, I want that tree more than anything in the world."

"Well, give me a dollar and it's yours," he said.

"What?"

"Give me a dollar and it's yours."

I could hardly hear that, I could've fallen flat on my face from joy and exhaustion, but I just stood there frozen, not with the cold, a gentle shove in the small of my back sent me towards this magnificent deep dark green Christmas tree that stood fully four-times my size. It was wide at the bottom and the sweep of the lower branches looked as if you could crawl onto just one of them and be cradled by the main branch, and be wrapped, or rather blanketed, by the limbs of the dark green sweet smelling pine. The branches were just far enough apart and staggered from the trunk of the tree as to give it the most luxurious body, tapering all the way to the top pinnacle where an angle could be placed to have an overview of the cascading branches below in all their dark green glory, liquid splendor. It was hard to believe that it was mine, so I just stood there looking at it. When I found my voice again, I turned to him and said, "I have two dollars, won't you please take at least that."

"Didn't I just teach you anything about giving?" he said to me, "if I take all your money, then you won't have anything to give anyone else, or do something else with it, that might give pleasure to others. Don't you get it yet?"

"I'll buy icicles with it, to trim the tree, make it shine in the light," I said.

"You could do that, or anything you wanted with it," he said, "You'll have it for anything else you may want. Don't you see?"

"I think so," I said.

"You better, or you're gonna be one sorry human being," he answered.

Then the thought occurred to me, "How was I gonna get it home?" With a startled look, I turned to him and said, "How am I going to get this home without hurting it?"

He said, "I thought you might be worried about that, once you got around to it. Believe me, it's a very strong tree and it can take more than you'd think. All you'd have to do is grab it from the strong low branches and drag it carefully through the snow on the sidewalk."

"The sidewalk's hard."

"The snow will act as a blanket and protect it."

"Are you sure it won't harm it?"

He laughed, "I'm sure."

"I wish I could be sure. I'll just die if anything happens to it, because it's just too beautiful to be hurt," I said in a rather awed hushed voice.

"You better hurry up and take it home now, because you're family's going to be worried about you, and it's Christmas Eve."

"Yes, and it's going to be the greatest Christmas ever, thanks to you," and with that, I did exactly as he said, and the amazing thing was that it felt so light dragging it along the sidewalks home.

I wasn't sure exactly which way home was, at this point, but I kind of trusted something else to guide me in what I thought was the general direction. My heart was filled with such joy, and was pounding with the thought of bringing it into the house and have everyone amazed at the perfection of such a tree. I had a feeling there might be some resistance to the presence of something that would shed needles or dirty the rug, making more work for my mother, but the dialog in my head had the answer, I said, "I'll do all the cleaning up and taking care of it, and you won't have to do a thing."

I went all the way home, and as I walked I imagined the dialog that would come at me and the answers I would give. I started rehearsing what I would say to anyone out loud on my way home, had anyone heard me, they would've thought maybe that I was nuts and call the police to take me away, but fortunately, there were few people out at this time. Of course I had no idea of where I was, all I knew was that it was dark and that I was going to catch hell from all sides. I counted on the tree to send them all in another direction and spare me the yelling, I was convincing myself that it didn't matter that the tree was a mode of getting presents, the symbol had, as its ultimate purpose, the venue of receiving gifts.

So many thoughts ran through my head, all having some validity to my mind, but through my head all having some validity that the overriding issue was on a belonging to the same race as my friends who would have trees in their houses. Eventually I came to the bare facts that the tree was a symbol of hope for me, a kid who wanted so much from life, and more than what I had experienced so far in this family, I chose somewhere along the line, I had a love for them that was deep and was unconditional.

Because my total understanding of them, and their journey, they had a different agenda from mine, which conflicted with what I had been taught with the family as one, that may be so in the most perfect of worlds, which I've come to understand is something to work towards, provided you get self interest out of the way, and I'm not sure you can, or even if you want to, since most discoveries and inventions, in my opinion, have as their aid more than a modicum of self-glorification and personal esteem. Oh well, that's life, and maybe that's as it should be. For now the most important thing was to get the tree home and up, and I truly began to feel it didn't matter what was under the tree, so long as that tree was there and I could admire it, and it would lend a grace to where I lived.

It was a symbol of faith, of hope, that things would get better in the lives of each of us, and I could go on dreaming of what would be possible for me when I grew up. Already I was thinking of how to put ornaments on it, to adorn it in some fashion, after all, people got dressed up for Easter and other holidays, so why shouldn't a tree get dressed up? I would see to it that something got done. Several times I looked back towards the lot and waved at the old man to who stood watching me go, and he waved back. Gradually he disappeared from sight, and as I rounded the corner things looked a little more familiar to me.

At one point I thought I heard someone talking to me, and I turned around rather frightened, as I hadn't passed anyone, I didn't see anyone in sight. I stopped in my tracks, "I could swear I could hear someone say something to me," I said to no one in particular. I was at once frightened and exhilarated, and a spurt of newfound energy propelled me towards my house, which I could now see was very close by. The thought of dragging into the house this magnificent tree was almost more than I could bear.

I started shouted half the way down the block, "I'm home, I'm home! Wait 'til you see what I've got! I'm home! I'm home, Mom! I'm home, Dad! I'm home everybody! Come, c'mon down, come and look! Help me, c'mon everybody!"

I burst through the side door like a gust of strong wind, screaming and shouting at my brothers to come and help me. My family was in the kitchen, having finished their dinner, obviously they got tired of waiting for me. The first words I heard from the kitchen were, in unison, "Where the hell have you been? We've called the police and everyone in the neighborhood."

There I was, at the bottom of the steps, with this huge tree lying just outside the door, as I could not get it through the doorway and the doorframe by myself. They were all bunched up at the top of the stairs, looking at me silently, and the tree, they stood dumbfounded. When they found their voices there was a cacophony of mixed questions, "Where'd you get such a huge tree? It'll never fit in the house. Did you take it off some lot?" All I could say was, "please help me get it in the house, and you'll see it will fit. I promise it will fit."

After all the commotion and everything settled down, when we had finally gotten it in the door, my mother and, of course with the rest of the family, asked the question again, "Where did you get that Christmas tree?" I looked at each one of them, and I saw their faces, their faces looked rather stunned in a way, and I heard my voice say to them, "I asked God for a favor."

After everybody had settled down, I had finally told them the whole odyssey of my search for a tree, and the kind of mystical experience, so to speak, that I had, finding a lot that I had never seen before, and the negotiations that ensued. They looked at me rather suspiciously and said, "Really?"

I said, "I swear to you, I swear to you on my grandmother's grave that is exactly what happened," and so finally they kind of believed me, and said, "Leave it to you."

I said, "I told you this year we were going to have a Christmas tree, and we were, and it's true, I did ask God for a favor, and he gave it to me." Now, no matter how many experiences we have in this life, the depth of the awareness of those specific moments, in retrospect, is always wanting, our judgment isn't always the best, and we fail so often to keep our own counsel. You see, I always seem to be a person who expected the sky to open up and pour down its bounty on me, whether it was a Christmas tree, no matter what it was, a paper route, a this, a that, whatever, I tried to listen for voices that would tell me what to do, what was next that I could expect, and more often than not, it would come about.

The Mind Is the Key

Neighborhoods always held something magical for me. Sitting on the steps of 624 Magnolia Street, the world would parade itself in front of me, and I loved people, and I loved always seeing them walk in very specific ways, and I guess I learned from my mother only to see the best in people. Growing up is hard in its judgment of what I wanted to believe, and that was really what was happening around me, dreaming continually, I continually dreamed.

Once I stopped dreaming, or put it aside with what we call reality, things would never be the same, the constant change made itself known, and that is not necessarily good, particularly for me. I am of an age now that reality is harmful, if not, in fact, deadening. I'll go back to dreaming. As I've stated, that I have at least started to return, to some degree, what I know is really me. My energy and will have returned stronger than ever, and daily, as I know that dreaming and energy are one, and without either, the world to accomplish is diminished, and death is not far off. I'll keep death at bay forever, and will only come as a surprise not worth the energy or the worry; one can live a very long time, if you set your mind to it.

The mind is the key in any belief system that bolsters every fact of the mind and its thinking process, so much to learn, so much to experience, so much to love, so much to cherish, it sits in waiting, only to be called on. I guess it's time to dig in to my memories again, and that seems to be stuck somewhere in this encapsulated body of mine, my mind, my inner-life, my inner-eye, the senses that see little beyond the six senses. Who knows? I for one don't.

Go back in time, my mind's time, where things seemed so simple, so pure, that it, at times, makes me want to cry. The thought of the smell of bread baking in the oven, my mother in the kitchen cooking meals four or five times a day, always for those who came in looking to feed themselves. Strange, it's all too painful, and for whom? Who cares? And yet the self-nagging voice in my head, "Write it down." There are so many lives that I've lived and they seem connected, and some seem disconnected, but they all are, in a strange way, connected.

I'm telling this memoir not in a linear sense, and it's kaleidoscopic, very much like the world. Even as my body has experienced them all at one time or another, in which time childish dreams that reverberate continually in my body, I'm limited by all my senses, as I'm told that science has discovered a world beyond the senses, and yet that is all I have to annotate this life that I'm living. As a two or three year old, I dreamed dreams and saw events that have colored my life ever since, where to begin.

Well, I've tried at the beginning, but then even that is rather sketchy, oranges and rose petals, rather sketchy. I remember that there was a time, I must have been about thirteen years old, when people would always come to the door, knock, and say, "Is Clifford home?"

My mother would say, "Yes,"

How Did You Know That?

And then they would say, "Can we see him?" and then they would come in and my mother would seat them comfortably in the living room, and they would begin to talk to me and tell me of their problems or troubles. I remember I was in camp one summer, and several people thought that they could consult me about anything, I have no idea as to why, none whatsoever, that people would ask or seek my counsel.

Here's a thirteen year old, what the hell could I have known at that time. However, I seem to kind of just spout stuff, and for whatever reason, however it happened, I seemed to somehow hit the mark for some of these people, and for most of them, they were seeking something and I supplied the answer, where that answer came from, I cannot tell you, I just simply talked, and said, "Well, blah blah blah blah blah blah blah."

And before you'd know it, they'd say, "Well, how did you know that?"

And I'd say, "I don't know, I just guessed it," and they somehow couldn't believe that a person could guess that. I could see myself in the living room, particularly with one young couple, and the girl had a clubfoot, she was at this summer camp that I was at, face was angelic beyond belief, and her boyfriend was just madly in love with her. They were questioning about the business of the clubfoot.

I said that, "In the light of things, that's not the issue here. Are you friends?",

And they said, "Of course we're friends."

"I mean, are you really friends?"

And they'd say, "Yes, I can't imagine a day without talking and being in the company of each other,"

I said, "Well, there's your answer. Do what you want, go ahead, but don't let that small impediment, large in the world, but small in your mind, don't let that affect you or your love for each other or your friendship."

Still, as we know, love lasts a certain length of time, and all of a sudden, people wake up and wonder what the hell has happened. Well, they forgot to be friends, real friends. One with whom one could speak and talk, and talk about "what's inside them"—communicate is the modern term—"somehow you can talk to each other and settle things in a way that is intelligent and loving."

People would come to the door constantly, and my mother would just look on and kind of smile, and I didn't know enough to ask her what she was thinking, I just assumed that they knew that somehow I knew something they didn't, whatever that is.

Graduating

As it seems, time has no real meaning for me, I don't think it ever has. Time is an enigma, as far as I'm concerned, and in high school things came rather easily. I graduated high school in a matter of two years because I had all kinds of things to do, they gave me credit for singing lessons, they gave me credit for whatever I did, I seemed to get a lot of credits, however it was.

Finally, one day, in the principal's office, Mr. Charles LeRoux at Woodward High School, said to me, " Clifford, you're graduating."

I said, "What?"

He said, "You're graduating. Come in to my office."

So, I went in to his office and he handed me a diploma, and he said, "Here, you've graduated. I've talked to Doctor Nash at the University of Toledo, and you're to be admitted this coming January," this was almost at Christmastime.

I looked at him and I said, "Are you sure?"

He said, "Yes, I'm sure. You don't belong here anyway, you'd better go to college."

He was an extraordinary man. I mean this principal was the model of all principal's, kind, thinking, generous, and bright beyond belief.

Come January, I went to Toledo University, met Doctor Nash, and he figured out a curriculum for me, according to Mr. LeRoux's direction, and I had all kinds of classes. I wasn't much enamored with the university, I didn't like university life because it seemed extraordinarily cliquish, people came in little groups, and somehow I always felt out of place.

So, I stayed for about six months and compiled about twenty-two units, and then at the end of it, I just simply went to Doctor Nash and thanked him, and said, "I'm going to New York, I need to leave Toledo, I need to start doing what I want to do." So, part of this narrative is the beginning of having gone to New York City, and that was quite an experience in the sense that I was sixteen years old and didn't have much college education.

§

NEW YORK CITY

Leaving Home

The leaving of my home and the members of my family that were very close and dear to my heart was as difficult a leave taking as ever I had imagined it could be. And yet I knew somehow that I couldn't continue to see myself settling down in the lifestyle that I knew in my heart was not true to what I dreamed was possible for me. Working in a factory was not my idea of living and being confined to a way of thinking and living that was not compatible with what I knew in the very fiber of my being as a satisfactory life without accomplishment of any kind acquiescing to the status quo.

I think at some time everyone confronts another part of their being and asked questions of themselves and if they didn't, something that occurs within them to change them as people in the community that they had no real desire to be a part of. If I may say, they turn themselves into very different people than what they originally were. Some become more discontented, blaming others for their inability to understand completely what was going on within themselves and as a result become destructive to those around, blaming others for the lack of responsibilities that they themselves acquiesced to. They very often miss the joy of life from the risk of failing.

For my own part, I think, painful though it may be, I've learned more by my failures. That doesn't necessarily mean that I stop questing for what I have in my mind's eye and what I know deep down is possible no matter how long it takes. It may take an entire lifetime; one hopes it doesn't but it may. And no matter what, giving up is not an option. What happens in my mind is that I can review with pictures, that is, pictures in my mind, in my imagination all the events that have happened to me. I have either the happy or unhappy coincidence of seeing things as they happen, advance in my life, come to my mind in pictures. It is both an advantage and sometimes a disadvantage but nevertheless it does exist, and to deny it would be a huge mistake, because I found in acting that what I had in my mind's eye eventually took place outside in the realm of reality—things that actually happened that I had dreamed would happen. My dreams became a reality.

It seems that when you let go of that dream in your mind's eye, you will abort what is possible. You relinquish that superior claim to reality. After all, the mind in my opinion is probably the most important gift that we have in order to succeed in the life of our own choice, and not somebody's idea of what is possible for us.

I believe it is the mantra of my own life that listening to other people and what they believe is possible is wrong—at least wrong for us and doesn't fit what we have in our mind. Our mind is the only thing that we really have that takes us to where we want to go, that keeps us alive, that keeps us thrilled with being alive.

I have found that, as far as I'm concerned, my life has had many different segments, each one containing a full story. The difficulty is finding out how they all fit with one another. The constant quest to improve on what already existed and to find a way to return to the very beginnings when I entered this life.

It seems a constant quest for that childlike state which knows no boundaries, no dictums, no opinions of others—that is, opinions as to opposing knowledge that others may impart. Again, one's mind is the governing force behind everything. That is, in my opinion the mind governs every moment in this life as long as it remains flexible and open to all venues of thinking and behaving, which is the result of thinking.

I Chose Acting

That point in my life in which I chose acting to bring together all the various parts of my life such as music, and the study of composition, of history, of art in the extreme—all came together in the world of acting, which ultimately deals with storytelling and the relationship of people with one another.

How they behave and what makes them unique is vital to assessing and bringing together, that is, bringing life to those ideas and hopefully sharing it with whomever would be interested. The search for who we are and what we have fantasized about our past and, yes, even the present fantasy as opposed to reality. More often than not reality is shoved aside in favor of fantasy—whether that is a mistake or not remains to be seen. In my opinion all things spring to life from the imaginative mind and every invention in this world started as a dream. I think we settle for a belief system within ourselves that either expands that state of imagination or contracts it. We have to be specific as to what we want for ourselves. If you have a picture in your mind's eye of what greatness is and can be, unless you be specific to the extent to which you want that greatness to extend itself—into either being seen by the world at large, or for whatever reason in not exposed. An incomplete belief system more often than not hampers the coming to fruition which we think we had hoped for. By not being specific to that dream, and I mean very specific, it forever remains in limbo, unaccomplished, things that have yet to be done—unfulfilled dreams that haunt the sub conscious.

Life Was an Education

I think life was more of an education for me. My brother Alex is the one who put me on the train one night, some time in September. I remember going down to Union Station and I had my winter coat and my brother Alex. I didn't want anybody else to go because everybody would be crying and I'd feel rotten, and I wasn't sure I wanted to go, and yet I knew I had to go.

It took my brother Alex to shove me a little, saying, "Go on, get going," to get me on the train, and I remember pulling out of the station, it must have been about eight-thirty, nine o'clock, and I would arrive the next morning in Grand Central Station.

I remember specifically, on the train, looking out the window, looking at all the city lights, and then the black when we'd go through the countryside, and the dark, and then all of a sudden a burst of lights of small towns along the way, and I would put my face out the window practically, and stare and look.

And then, I think, well I know, I started to cry, and I didn't want anybody to see me, but I cried, and I was beginning almost immediately to become homesick. I thought, "C'mon, this is an adventure, and you've always loved adventures, and this is gonna be a great one," so finally having convinced myself it was going to be great, I came out of this funk and fell asleep, and the next morning I woke up in Grand Central Station.

Forgive me if this is redundant, but I remember when I got into the station with my bag, there was a conductor in the middle of the floor who looked at me and said, "What you want is the Travelers Aid," and at that time there was a woman who sat behind the desk with a white cap, she looked like a nurse.

He said, "Go over and talk to that lady and she'll tell you just how to maneuver and go through the city like you know it."

I went up to her and I told her why I was here, and she said, "Well, young man, if you'll just have a seat," and I sat down. She picked up the phone and called the YMCA, 5 West 63rd Street, and she said, "I have a young man here, blah blah blah blah blah, and he needs a room," so they said, "just send him over."

So, finally, she said, "You're going to go to 5 West 63rd Street, the YMCA. Now, at the front of this building, in front of Grand Central Station, is a bus that'll take you right to the door," as it did practically.

I got on the bus, paid the fare, and went into the YMCA.

The man at the desk said, "Ah, you're the young man that so-and-so spoke about, the Travelers lady," and he said, "We have a room for you at this time. It'll be twelve dollars a week."

Well, I had sixty dollars on me, and that was five weeks if I didn't eat, and they had a cafeteria downstairs where our food was, very good, reasonable—not great food, but adequate, and I would have to stay with two guys from Brazil in a big room, and it turned out to be two weeks rather than a couple of days. So here I was, with these two Brazilian guys who really spoke very little English, but they were nice enough and, in fact, very kind. Sensing that I was just a kid and feeling rather scared, they invited me to have dinner with them in the downstairs cafeteria. We managed the English and they clued me in on the workings of the Y, take a shower early in the morning or late at night, talk to very few people, be nice and friendly, but not too friendly.

As I learned the ropes, when I walked down the hall to the lavatory, one of the guys had a door that was always open, and usually sat with three or four other guys talking about and discussing art and music and pretty much anything possible. The guy whose room it was loved talking and he was very verbal, he let it be known that he was Jewish and smart as hell, so get your facts straight and be intelligent in conversation. He was always ragging on me and talking about the New York Times, his favorite saying was "the model of the New York Times is all the news that fits we print."

He was very funny, and he made no bones about being gay, and once I let it known that I was not interested or inclined, he let up on the innuendos and engaged me in intelligent and very enlightening conversations. He always had a glass of wine in his hand, he arrived at 6 pm, and he "held court," so to speak, and from time to time it could be fun. He teased me about hanging onto the doorframe, "I'm not gonna bite you," he said.

"No, no no," I said, "I'm fine, I'm fine." I had to have a job and quickly, sixty dollars doesn't go very far and it doesn't last very long.

I remember that when I was in Toledo my uncle had guests from New York, and they told me, "Anytime you come to New York, we'd love to hear from you, blah blah blah blah," and so I said, "Okay," and then the next morning I called Mrs. DePace.

Michael DePace was an impresario, he represented opera singers, and Mrs. DePace said to me, "We have a friend who's name is Rita Sorrentino, and she will interview you if you're looking for a job."

I said, "absolutely," so I went there. I went in and made an appointment, she was the head lady for the boys who delivered stocks and bonds and checks to Wall Street for Texaco Oil. Rita Sorrentino was her name, I'll never forget it, she was extraordinary. She was kind, lovely, and of course, because they were friends with Mrs, DePace, she was particularly kind to me.

I was offered the job instantly, and she said, "Can you start work tomorrow?"

And I said, "absolutely." The pay was, at that time, twenty-eight dollars a week, and that was considerable in a way, not great, but you can manage to live on that at twelve dollars a week, sixteen dollars a week with eating, and if you work overtime they give you a little bit more money. So, I started doing that, and that was the beginning of my New York sojourn.

A Few Years Later

I'm gonna push forward ahead, and later on I'll figure out how to put it together. It's several years beyond the period of when I first came to New York City and worked for Texaco Oil Company,

I finally went to a conservatory and there I met someone who steered me in another direction, which was the acting direction, and this section concerns Marilyn Monroe and Marilyn at The Actors Studio. I've resisted writing, or telling this story of how we met and began to work, all too briefly with her.

I became a member of The Actors Studio in 1962; I was given the privilege of a life membership after a series of two grueling auditions. The procedure then was, one picked a scene, or a piece of material, an acting scene, lasting no longer than five minutes, and you were asked to bring material with a partner, and audition before a group, say six to twelve, who were already members.

They would judge you on a particular day or evening, as the case may be, and you would perform your work, and after which time you were notified that either you had passed the first audition or you were asked to come back.

If you passed it, you were deemed worthy of auditioning for Lee Strasberg, Elia Kazan, and Cheryl Crawford. Now, they were the heads of the Studio and they all had to agree that you were worthy of becoming a member.

They had to agree that you were sufficiently talented to be admitted, and as a lifetime member, they were very careful, and it must have been only two or three people at most per year who got in. The Actors Studio on W. 44th Street, between 9th and 10th Avenues was in actuality a church that no longer functioned as a church. It was gutted so that the upstairs was a vast space rising some 40 feet in height with the surrounding balcony. The acting space was large, so that it could accommodate risers of every size to make a stage that rose some three feet off the floor. Huge beams stretched across the room and opened the ceiling that gave the acting space enormous size.

First Audition

I was called to prepare myself and my partner to go up the sidesteps that led into the room. There were seven rows of chairs and each row was elevated above the preceding one, stadium design. The stairwell was dark, and so coming into the room was slightly startling. I had the lights for the scene lowered, to give the effect of a room in an ante-bellum mansion. A library in fact, with Joanna seated at a desk lit by candlelight. It was the first thing I wanted the members of the committee to see. I had Joanna preceding me as I came up the back stairs and approached the room as if by huge hall doors. I moved into a lowlight that illuminated my presence. It was as if two pools of light featured us both. As I approached Joanna from behind her desk chair, the room was still, and deathly still. Joe Christmas looks Caucasian but in fact is black.

I stood still for about a full minute before uttering the first line of the scene: "Good evening, Joanna"! She was startled, then composed herself to reply, "Good evening, Joe." From there, the scene slowly developed into a whiplash of open confrontation using my shirt as a whip. There I was, bare-chested in low-cut pants that hung by my hips. I was six feet tall and weighed some 160 pounds. Very muscular. I had oiled my chest and arms so that they glistened as if by sweat from a hot and sultry night in the South. The scene became a culmination of the prior dance with sexual overtones, by each of them at different times during his employment by Joanna, as manager of her plantation and cotton fields. The scene seemed to go well, as both Joanna and Joe fairly bristled with sexual constraint until the high arc of the scene exploded violently.

After we had finished the scene, I took my partner Joanna out for dinner to access and discuss the work we had just done. I thanked her profusely and told her as soon as I hear from the studio I will let her know. I asked her if she wanted to be included in this scene as her audition as well is mine? She answered she would rather wait until Lee signaled it was time for her to do a scene on her own. I couldn't argue with that, so the night ended with, "I'll call you as soon as I hear from the studio, would that be all right?"

She answered, "Let me know and I'll be there." And with that she gave me a kiss on the cheek and said, "I will hold all the thoughts for you, you should be proud that the scene went wonderfully well, and I have a feeling that you passed!"

I answered, "From your mouth to God's ears," and with that I walked home, my mind racing all the while, going over the scene constantly, over and over again. It took me until 4 am to finally fall asleep, dreaming constantly of the scene.

At 11 am the next morning I got a call from the Actors Studio office, and the voice on the other end said, "Congratulations, you just passed the first audition and Lee, Elia and Cheryl Crawford will see you in two weeks doing the same scene. Don't change anything, and good luck"! Two weeks? What the hell am I going to do in two weeks? A voice in my head answered, "Rehearse, ass hole." Keep working!

I called Joanna with the good news and she said, "When do we rehearse?" I answered, "Would this afternoon be okay?" "You bet," was her answer.

The Actors Studio

The misconception that The Actors Studio was a school for the study of acting is completely false. It was started, as I was told, by Elia Kazan and a director by the name of Bobby Lewis, as a place for professional actors to work and develop their talent and material that interested them, and which may or may not be true to their type, or would even be cast as it.

Stretching their talent was the ultimate goal, stretching their talent to the outer limits, work against type. In my case, to play a dockworker or a street hood, as opposed to Richard III or Lord Byron.

In that time, the group may have consisted of about thirty or forty Broadway actors, that included Marlon Brando, Montgomery Clift, Geraldine Page, Maureen Stapleton, and so many, many more, all recognizable names. I believe it was 1947 that The Actors Studio was started, and it was a laboratory of how an actor developed and expanded their talent. It was only later, as I understood it, that Lee Strasberg was brought in to head and critique their work.

There is a whole world of how that all came about, a book written by Harold Clurman on the group theatre, to which Lee Strasberg, Elia Kazan, and Cheryl Crawford were the heads, as well as Harold Clurman and so many more. They formed a company afterwards called Group Theatre. Writers, like Clifford Odets would write specific works for them to perform, and in some cases those plays were produced on Broadway, such as Golden Boy, Waiting For Lefty, and many more.

In California

I was in California in the 1950's, working as a pageboy for CBS. I made the acquaintance of several up-and-coming young directors, such as Arthur Penn, Jack Smith, and Bob Mulligan. For some reason, I don't remember how, but somehow I was invited to come to somebody's house to help read a new play, as it became known that I had hoped to be an actor and work in the movies or television or, in fact, anywhere.

After the reading, it seemed that Arthur Penn was impressed enough to say to me that I should be in New York, and working or studying with Lee Strasberg. He would ask Lee to see me, and then decide whether he would take me as a student in his professional classes. The fact that I had already been in New York from Toledo, Ohio at the age of sixteen proved no difficulty for me. I knew New York well by that time.

Do I digress and tell the New York part of the story? My God, this gets more circuitous than ever.

Short Digression

I had a cousin who was by nature a mover and a shaker, and who by sheer dint of will, and ambition, took over her father's failing cardboard box company, to make it a huge success, by clearing the field of her four brothers. A sister was an ally in the scheme of taking over the whole business—suffice to say, she did, and I mean she went at it like a tigress. She slept in her car in Washington D.C., this was during the war. She stormed her way into her Massachusetts congressman's office to try to get a war contract from the government for her box business, shipping materials and etc. I can't begin to write of the story that made her life, ultimately, a huge success, such a success, that she ultimately sold the company to Olivo Hansford and also became an important board member of that company.

Along the way, she brought to Toledo this man, an important opera impresario and his wife to visit and spend time in Toledo, to meet with my uncle, my father's brother, who happened to be, at that time, the Metropolitan Bishop of the Eastern Orthodox Church. Mary Dowd was her name, she was a distant cousin and she became a staunch advocate for my uncle as possible leadership, and even as much as being a Patriarch of the whole Eastern Orthodox Church in the world, Mexico, America, and Canada. My uncle was probably the most preeminent, I guess you'd call him a cantor, of the Byzantine vocal music in the world.

As a matter of fact, all the male members of my family, going back many, many, generations, everyone had a voice, and they were known for their voices, and so I having one as well, seemed to be the next inheritor of the singing aspirations of being a priest.

This was made known to the impresario and his wife, who said, "If you're ever in New York, please look us up"—

and I already told you about Rita Sorrentino. Needless to say, I did it that fall, and as I arrived in New York at Grand Central Station, I had very little money in my pocket.

Rita Sorrentino was a blonde northern Italian, with a statuesque body, beautiful, extraordinarily beautiful woman, and a no-nonsense person. She told me to come the next day, and she explained where she was, she was on 42nd Street on the 47th floor of the Chrysler Building, and it was at 42nd and Lexington. She told me to take the bus on Broadway at 64th Street, and it would take me to 42nd Street where I'd catch the crossstown and get off at 42nd and Lex.

When I walked into the lobby of the Chrysler Building, it was as if I had stepped into the Grand Canyon. Marble all over the place, beautiful inlaid floors, it was as beautiful an Art Deco building as one could possibly imagine. Information directed me to the bank of elevators specifically for Texaco Oil, and it would take me to the floor on which the receptionist was, and the receptionist would direct me to the office of Rita Sorrentino. I walked down a long corridor and eventually I arrived at a door that had printed on it "Mail Room." I went in there and there was a room full on young guys seated around a table, and before that, I walked up to the office with glass windows revealing Rita Sorrentino seated at her desk.

I knocked on the door, and she said, "Come in." I was nervous as hell; would she like me, was I dressed properly? I'd put on the only suit that I had and a shirt and tie, which I rarely ever wore, and I felt like a schoolboy, ushered into the principal's office. She stood up, held out her hand, and had this radiant smile on her face, a completely very kind look.

"Sit down," she said, and I sat opposite her. She put me at ease quickly and asked me how I knew the DePace's. I told her of my meeting them in Toledo, and then she asked me why I had chosen to come to New York.

I told her I wanted to study singing and possibly acting, but for now I needed a job to support myself and gradually pay for lessons, and then from there, I wasn't sure. First things first, I needed a job.

She said, "Okay, well, you have one, and it pays twenty-eight dollars a week. Could you manage on that?"

"Of course I could," I said. She asked me where I was staying, and I told her about the Y on 5 West 63rd Street. What was my rent? I told her twelve dollars per week.

She said at certain times, when I was bonded, I could earn a bit more, but first I had to learn the subway systems. She said that I could accompany one of the boys there until I learned where the banks were, and the offices, and what I would need to know, and where the checks would be deposited at the bank, and the official papers that needed to be delivered to the people directly responsible for those letters. She thought I would learn quickly and then she would assign me certain deliveries that were priorities, and those paid more.

Did I know New York? You bet, most of the runners were New Yorkers.

Arthur Penn had given me Lee's telephone number, Lee Strasberg, and said, "When you get to New York, call him. And when you get settled, ask for an appointment."

I left California, as I was there first, directly for New York and the Y, yes they had the room. I called Lee's office, actually it was his apartment, and they told me that I could have an appointment, and that Arthur Penn had already spoken to them.

I was greeted by a secretary who ushered me into the library. Here was this rather short man with thinning white hair and a rather reserved smile. He extended his hand and then pointed to a chair to take a seat.

He asked if I had studied before, and I proceeded to tell him no, but I had attended the Manhattan School of Music, and studied voice, composition, and some piano. That seemed to impress him, in a way, maybe not immensely, but I think he was impressed. He questioned me about music from my standpoint of compositions, conductors, pianists, etc. He asked me why I wanted to study acting, and I remember telling him that I had always wanted to act, to be an actor, for as long as I could remember.

Theory of Childhood Events

I would like to continue this theory that I have stated before in this memoir and that is, the event or events that take place in one's childhood. And by that I mean either one or many traumatic situations or occurrences that take place from the age of 0 to 10 or 11 years of age.

My earliest recall was hearing my uncle the Archbishop sing the liturgy of the Church during the mass in the Eastern Orthodox church. Most members of my family either in the past or present were gifted with voices and so it was that I had and still have a voice. There was in me—either acknowledged or suspected—a competition with my uncle. My voice from the earliest years had a beauty as a boy soprano, and also during the change that inevitably went through the necessary change from boy soprano to the adult male voice. That change would create difficulties throughout my adult life.

My voice was quixotic to say the least. It would go from bass to tenor depending on the day and the vocalizing that took place. Rather late in life a major doctor of vocal expertise would diagnose my vocal chords as extra long, thereby creating a certain amount of difficulty. Vocal cords have to come together perfectly in order to create sound. Certain illnesses at one point in my life caused physical problems both in the lungs and the vocal cords—and so it was that I had to physically create the perfect muscular strength and perfection required to make the proper tone.

Through several years of hard work, I eventually brought my vocal chords back to their original capabilities. They were always a consideration in my career as a singing actor and singer. I never entered a musical but that my secret concern for my voice was among the most consideration given to the musical score and the execution that I was required to make in any role I was contracted to perform. If one looks closely at that condition it can seem like a highly temperamental artist, but in fact and in honesty it was fear that held me back at very crucial times. If one looks at the major works that I have performed on Broadway and elsewhere it would seem to others that there was no difficulty in the least, but merely artistic temperament.

If one can look at this condition logically and in depth it can reveal itself for what it really is and that is a basic distrust that my voice would perform as I envisioned it and heard it in my head. When it was functioning as I had rehearsed it, it could be thrilling—as many critics in the theater had written about me.

It was a secret that I kept very close to myself. Only now am I sure of the ability to perform anything I chose to execute. My motto has always been that "it is never too late to achieve what I knew was possible for me." I believe there will come a time when I will be given the opportunity to display what are my natural gifts. Only time will tell and the possibility of achievement will show itself.

So, in reading this memoir one will see opportunities accepted and those that were denied by me through the fear that I'd had in the past. I had a psychiatrist tell me that I would never truly rid myself of fear and that I would have to learn how to handle it, I believe I have learned.

Lee Strasberg

I told him that as a kid I'd do plays in the basement of my home, plays that usually involved being a king, or play-acting scenes of revenge or whatever. I learned a lot from going to the movies; the movie house was actually my schooling. In fact, from about the age of eight, or even younger, I could be found on Sunday afternoons seated in a seat at the Mystic Theatre in Toledo, Ohio, and stay there forever, it seemed, throughout the same movie two or three times, Flash Gordon, Errol Flynn as Robin Hood, Charles Laughton as Henry VIII, Norma Shearer as Marie Antoinette, and so on; it seemed costume dramas from other centuries fascinated me the most, although Stella Dallas with Barbara Stanwyck being one of the exceptions, anything with high drama.

After listening to me for a while he said he would take me, but I'd have to wait a week or so. I was to call him again next week and his secretary would tell me which class I was to attend. In a high state of energy and excitement, I left his apartment. The day was, I believe, a Thursday, 11am to 7pm, that was the time assigned to me. His studio at that time was a small theatre right above a movie house on 50th Street and Broadway, it was the perfect space for acting. It was wide, six rows deep, Lee sat in the front row and commenced to conduct the class in sense-memory work, the idea gleaned from Stanislavski's method of training an actor.

I had already read My Life and Art, and was somewhat familiar with the method as developed by Stanislavski to train actors of the Moscow Art Theatre. In order to train actors to achieve a like-level of acting work, Stanislavski studied the acting of the then greats, like Eleanora Duse, Salvini, Chiappe, and so many more—those were considered great, great actors, great singers.

One thing in common with all of them was the use of

their imaginations, effective memory concerning events in their lives of transforming, of transformative nature, episodes and sense memory.

I would learn from so many books on the theatre, Harold Clements book on the group theatre, Boleslawski's Seven Lessons On Acting, Michael Chekhov's work with actors, and Stanislavski's major pupil, Vakhtangov and his theatre work. Three of New York's finest acting teachers went to Russia to work with Stanislavski at the Moscow Art Theatre. As I was to learn later, each took from Stanislavski the part of his work that impressed them the most.

Three Approaches to Acting

With Lee, it would be the work of Freud, from a psychological viewpoint, plus sense memory, the idea that as we grow older our senses become dulled and we no longer experience life from a complete and full sensory position as we once did as babies or children. A child being less constrained by convention and society, they are free to react and behave fully with few constraints dictated by adult and familial requirements, experience smell as if for the first time, and so on with optimum experience of the five senses, and occasionally the sixth sense.

Stella Adler, as I recall, was more involved with the imagination side of Stanislavski's work, free to roam and be able to associate freely, in an experiential way, the results of imagination, the life around the characters in the play, and the full use of the polygonal being, what if and so on.

Sandy Meisner took, I believe, the repetitious part of speech and listening, and as if one had to really listen so that they heard and really took in what was being said, perhaps the seventh time speech and communication finally sinks in and the listener finally hears and experiences the full implications of was being said, and physically feels the impact of what has been communicated by one individual or many individuals to each other.

I will not presume to fully comprehend the methods of the latter two, but as for Lee Strasberg, I can vouch for the extraordinary responses to the senses, sense memory and the exercises that I experienced in my work, also affective memory.

My studies as an actor with Lee Strasberg proved how vital seeing, smelling, and tasting is, and I use the word vital in the most important sense to describe what makes an actor completely different from every other actor. I love greatness in anything, and the blessing that it bestows on the owner and the listener and everyone who comes in contact with them, although does anyone really own it. It, to my mind, is a search to be alive and to extend the number of years one has to keep it close, even as a part of the bloodstream that courses through the entire body, greatness is something that I'm not sure is an inherited trait, if it's given at birth, or if it develops over time by the seeker, is it an insane quest, or does it steal upon an individual, like so much fog that covers the body. One mustn't look for affirmation from others, or so called critics, it just is what it is, it isn't kind or considerate of others. Or, does it seep, when it happens, like a drug, an obsession that seeps into the person's soul who seeks it.

Affective Memory

Affective memory exercises on emotional experiences one may have had in life, not by the result or the impact of that traumatic experience, but the event or the sensory aspect of it leading up to that event. That is an important and very essential response to say that the heat of the day, the smell of the atmosphere, the sight of the room, or tenant surroundings, sensory in the extreme that things to life of a specific want that may or may not have caused a traumatic block.

Scientists have since agreed that smell is one of the truly affecting senses of things past or even hidden. When I taught, I had a student whose physical experience of smell brought such total and traumatic response that it was unbelievably difficult for her to contain and she ran out of the room and went probably into the bathroom. The smell somehow brought back the physical punishment administered to her by her parents for her behavior, and that to them was not acceptable, no matter what the emotional damage was being done to her, so much so, as I said, she ran out of the studio and threw up in the ladies' room.

When she returned to class, she said the experience for her was one of complete unpleasant recall, an experience she had forgotten, or repressed, in her subconscious. Later, she said it freed her of a deep resentment toward her family and the feelings of past emotions related to this experience. I didn't press her further, but encouraged the forgiveness aspect of this traumatic experience.

We forget how powerful the senses really are in the very beginning of our lives. Watch a baby go through the development of touch, smell, seeing, tasting, things always go into the mouth, and all kinds of developing sensory feelings are explored with no exceptions.

Auditioning

As I went to his class, I learned that Lee had instructed the class-secretary not to accept money from me anymore, but that I was required to attend the class five days a week, in all four sessions of his teaching. After two years Lee approached me and said, "Isn't it about time you started auditioning for The Actors Studio?" It was more than a hint, so I immediately went about finding a suitable scene, as only a five-minute audition piece, and I hit upon the idea of extracting a scene from "Light In August" by Faulkner, a rather violent scene between Joe Christmas and Joanna, his employer, highly charged and overtly loaded sexuality. In our rehearsals of approximately six weeks, I came up with a behavior of removing my shirt and using it as an extension of my body, almost as a whip, the ultimate arousal of Joanna into a fight and a mode, a mode that seemed animalistic, almost in the extreme in both of us, not so much overtly, but smoldering separately until the episode was about ready to explode. In the day of the audition I came first to go around. I was nervous beyond belief, and I tried to relax and concentrate deeply on the experience yet to come.

I was called the next day and was told that I had passed the first round, and that my next and final audition would be before Lee Strasberg, Elia Kazan, and Cheryl Crawford—all three had to agree on admittance at the time. The Actors Studio had occupied a preeminent position in the world of acting. It was a highly visible and current state of acceptance by everyone in the entertainment world; Marlon Brando, Montgomery Clift, Jimmy Dean, Geraldine Page, Maureen Stapleton, Eli Wallach, you name it. They were all considered the cream of the acting world and they were a part of The Actors Studio.

At that time, 1960, there were approximately one hundred and fifty lifetime members. Once you passed the finals, you were admitted without cost as a lifetime member. The audition period was a grueling experience, and emotions ran high by all of us. Acceptance into this group was an assured open door into the world of the theatre, movies, and television. Needless to say, the doubt that one had as to the talent was always at the forefront of every working moment. Am I gifted? Will they see what I can offer? Will they want to see me in my work? Will they understand and feel what I want them to feel and to experience in my work?

Every possible emotion dealing with the acceptance lay at the bottom of every action and interaction. It was a frightening and heady time. I waited along with six other pairs of finalists, and rarely was there more than two finalists chosen to become life members during that year. Will one of them be me?

It just so happened that I lived in a coldwater building on 46th Street between 9th and 10th Avenue at that time, and after class with Lee, I went walking around Hell's Kitchen, as it was then known, looking to see if an apartment would become available. It so happened that a sign was displayed at 451 West 46th Street, "Super wanted, call Mr. Heitmann for inquiries." I called immediately and got a nice, but tough-sounding guy on the other end of the phone. He asked if I could meet him at 4 pm at 451 West 46th Street.

"I'll be there," I said.

There he was, standing in front of the red brick building waiting for me a little before 4 pm. I shook hands with him, he had a firm grip and a no-nonsense attitude. He said, "C'mon in and let me show you the Super's apartment." The stench of the cat piss permeated the wooden floors in the hallway so that it about nearly knocked me over. He said, "this is a coldwater building. The duties of the Super are to mop the halls and take out the garbage. Here is the basement, but no heating furnaces."

To the left of the door after the entrance was a door that said "Super" on it. Mr. Heitmann opened the door and it led immediately into the kitchen, a standing open washtub stood beside the door and the living room. In the living room were two windows that looked out on 46th Street. To the right was a room, the bedroom, and a small door that was a toilet room. Period. No washstand, nothing. You washed your hands in the kitchen sink that stood beside a four-burner gas stove, that in fact that was the purpose for the heat of the apartment and the means of boiling water for your bath and other cleaning.

He looked at me said, "Your rent is free and you get eighty-three dollars a month as wages."

The first thing I asked was, "Who pays for the Pine Sol?"

"Pine sol?" he says.

"Yes," I said, "for mopping the halls."

A slight pause, and then he looked at me and said, "Okay, we'll buy you Pine Sol. How much do you want?"

I said, "four gallons."

He looked at me and he said, "four gallons?"

"Yes. These halls have to be cleaned thoroughly and to get the cat piss stink out of the building."

He hadn't realized just how clean I intended the halls to be, and the walls in the place were to be cleaned beyond belief, so much so that the paint would probably come off. It became a running joke, "do you own stock in Pine Sol?" he said.

You see, for a few months I must've used more than fifty gallons of disinfectant, and I kept the front hall door open and the back door open, that led out into a small backyard. The wind would whip through the halls enough to stop neighbors and passers-by to comment, "Where the hell is that pine smell coming from."

Needless to say, I took the job. Mr. Heitmann hadn't figured I was a health nut and a cleanliness nut, but I had inherited it from my mother—she would be on her hands and knees in the corners of our house, cleaning, scraping every inch of our floors clean, so that you could eat off the floor.

No shoes were allowed. They were left at the side door, and then you were permitted to enter the house. There were plastic covers over everything, to protect the fabric of the chairs, couch, and Persian rugs. I used to tease her, "the house that plastic built."

"Quiet," she'd say, "You want to live in a dirty house?" and then she would laugh this lovely high, musical kind of giggle and then full-throated laughter would come.

I would kiss her and give her a huge hug, "There is no on like you, Mom."

So you see, I came by this cleanliness thing quite naturally, something Mr. Heitmann hadn't figured on, in the beginning.

Once engaged, I commenced tearing down the dirty plaster on the walls, exposing the red-brick walls which, eventually, I brushed with linseed oil to bring out the red in the bricks, painted the floors black, and the trim white, if I was going to live here, it was going to be as spotlessly clean as I could get it. The black floors looked shellacked, I mean to a fare-thee-well.

I eventually furnished the apartment with good, used furniture and a bed bought from the Salvation Army Store over on 45th Street and 11th Avenue, the apartment finally took shape.

I attended Lee's class four days a week, 11 am to 1 pm, and in between classes, and rehearsals for scenes, I read everything in sight, and then I also had the chores of being a Super; life was busy as hell.

Eventually, I filled the building with actors, singers, dancers, writers, anyone who aspired to be something and chose to live their dream.

Many a night, we'd have one or two people yelling down the hallway, "Spaghetti anyone? Bring the wine!" I'm reminded of an incident with a butcher, very early on after I first moved into the neighborhood, a butcher on 9th Avenue. You could walk all the way down 9th Avenue to 37th or 36th Street, and on either side were markets of all kinds, markets for vegetables, for fish, for meat, everything, Italian grocers, Greek import stores, vegetable open-air stalls, and a veritable bazaar unlike any place else in New York City.

Between 44th and 45th Street there was this particular butcher shop known as Pitchuneenee. In the window was this huge azalea plant, spread out over the entire window, something like eight or nine feet, it always seemed to be in full flower, just beautiful. I peeked through the window to see there were four large butcher blocks with a chair in front of each of them. Behind these blocks were various butchers occupied with cutting meat and such, and behind the first block stood a rather elegant-looking man in a white coat and a Tyrolean hat with a pheasant feather jutting backwards out of it, it seemed to be about two feet long. He had a small goatee and a white face, a beautiful, wonderfully carved face, a kind of Rembrandt face.

I decided to go in, and it looked expensive, but what the hell, nothing ventured, nothing gained. I sat down in front of him, and watched him flatten out several pieces of pale meat.

I asked him, "Excuse me, what is that?"

He looked up at me and said, "Veal."

"Looks good," I said. He just nodded. "I think I'll have a piece of that," I said.

"No, no, no, I don't think so," that was his answer.

"No, no, no? Well, why? Is that all you have," I asked.

"No, I have more, but not for you." I was puzzled, is he being rude? I didn't think so, but then why that answer?

"Why not?"

"Too expensive, and not really nourishing," he said this in a kind of soft Italian accent.

"Well, okay, then how about a piece of inexpensive steak?"

He kept on flattening this piece of veal, and spreading it neatly between immaculate white butcher paper.

"No, I don't think so."

Well, I began to wonder what the hell is going on here. He looked up at this young guy, me, on the thin side, possibly looking like a poet of sorts, definitely a student aura about me.

"Chicken," he said.

"Chicken?" That's what I answered, "chicken?"

"Yes chicken, cheap, a dollar twenty-five a pound and very nourishing."

"Chicken?" I repeated.

"Put it in a pan with a little olive oil, a little salt and pepper, fry it, and then, if you want, add some crushed tomatoes and basil, maybe some olives and an onion, very delicious and nourishing," and without further ado, he walked into this big cooler and brought out a beautiful chicken. He removed the liver and quartered the chicken, wrapped it up in wax paper, then butcher paper, and handed it to me.

"One dollar and twenty-five cents, please," and a big smile on his face, "You'll do better with this," he said, "and if you don't have the other items, fry it, and it'll be very good, very good tasting, and good for you."

This began a friendship, and I cannot tell you, the memory of it is just delicious, the ritual of chicken. As I was handed the chicken, I knew it felt more than a pound in weight.

I looked at him, he started back and said, "see you next time."

Then and there began a friendship of respect and kindness, one I shall never forget, and one friendship that I shall never experience in quite the same way again.

For whatever reason, I was to receive my whole life help, kindness, and opened doors into a world I could only have dreamed about in the beginning of my career. I will not go into the difficulties and the psychological awareness of myself at various times, I'm not always as smart as I would've hoped to be.

It seems no matter what advantages I was given, a talent would always seem to be not far away, fear never to be conquered, and was with it, the challenges at hand seemed to be irrevocably tied together, joined until death do us part.

It has been said just how difficult of a person Lee Strasberg had been, and how destructive his teaching could be, and how cruel his critiques on the work would be. I can only say from my point of view, and vantage point, this was in fact not so.

His view of a career in acting was demanding, and he knew difficult, and how difficult would be, and quixotic personalities that could make or break careers, how one minute you could be on top of the world, and the next you could be discarded and shoved aside, ignored completely, and live for many years with that rare possibility of a supreme comeback.

His belief in talent as the only sure answer, and the constant discipline of work on one's instrument, as he referred to us, as actors, and the enigmatic amalgam of what goes in to making an actor. personalities play a part in the mystery of why actors can affect audiences, but that is, in my opinion, an ephemeral and minor component. It's high school popularity, that awful aging of a beautiful woman that, in the final years, borders on the ugly.

I've always been a juvenile, and probably will always remain so. We see and experience so little of greatness in acting, and almost every other field, that at times, we don't even experience it when it's right in front of us.

Not the least of what makes a great actor is the drama that writers put before us. The situations that they create, such as Shakespeare, the language of it, the stories he tells in the language, and both, foreign and familiar. The challenge is to bring to life the dreams in one's head, the imaginary vision that meets in concrete equivalence outside the mind and the body, that flesh, that shapes a vision for all to experience in our own unique way. That's what happens when two people come away with the same emotional response to a work of art, a play, a symphony, from any art form—each person has the experience, and feels the experience differently, and rightly so, as they are different for each of us. It is when there are more people than not, who come away from that artistic experience somewhere in the ballpark of what the writer intended; there is a consensus of the responses that come to bear.

Isn't It About Time?

It was somewhere between two and three years of intense study that Lee came up to me and said, "Isn't it about time you've thought about the auditioning process for The Actors Studio?" and I really didn't have an answer for that, so he went away, and didn't give me time to really think, he just laid it at my door step.

He said, "you need a haircut for the meeting I've set up for you, so go to see this barber." He handed me a paper with an agent's name and phone number below the barber's name and address. The agent's name was Edie Van Cleve at MCA, a legendary name in the field of talent agencies. She represented some of the most recognized talents in the field of entertainment, some were close to being great.

Now began the search for an audition scene, a partner, and six-week period of constant rehearsal. In between the meeting with Edie Van Cleve, who immediately set about lining me up with auditions, within a few weeks I was auditioning all over the place, and handed a role in a TV extravaganza entitled "The Fifth Column" starring Richard Burton and Maximilian Schell, directed by none other than, John Frankenheimer.

In the cast was a guy named Sydney Pollack; we became friends, not great friends, but friends. Who knew what he was to become, the Sydney Pollack, extraordinarily gifted, and of course he went on to produce and act in the highest level of the entertainment world. He knew how to work the system and he was gifted, the two go hand-in-hand.

We started rehearsing and all seemed to be going very well. Richard, that is Richard Burton, invited me to have drinks after rehearsal, little did I realize I was, and would be, no match for this drinking machine, a brilliant raconteur and an unbelievably well-read person.

One day after a couple of weeks of intense rehearsals, we went for drinks at the local bar and we sat on stools aside each other, and then he brought out a brown paper bag containing, what I was to discover after he told me to open it.

I said, "For me?"

He said, "Yes," and then took a big slug of drink. The package contained a two-volume set of Prefaces to Shakespeare by Harley Granville-Barker. I was completely taken aback and, needless to say, thrilled.

He said, "Ya know, you really are suited to Shakespeare."

"Am I?" I said.

He looked at me rather strangely and said, "Of course, and you know that. You know, you need to get to work and study."

If memory serves me correctly, I hung my head and I nearly started to cry. He reached his arm over my shoulders and said, "Welcome." I never understood what that word would ultimately come to mean, and I mean really mean.

Never Truly at Ease

I can honestly confess that I have never been truly at ease in a group of actors in a play or otherwise, and a few rare moments on the stage, to this day, I have rarely felt I had done the kind of work I am, and was, capable of doing. Laertes, naturally in Hamlet, came close and Hamlet was even closer, but it never came to fruition because of British Equities rules, even though the great English director Martin Webster went to bat for me in London—the story of Lord Olivier to come later for me to tell you about.

A few days later Edie called me and said, "You have an audition for a play called Caligula by Albert Camus with Sidney Lumet directing."

I went to the theatre on 53rd Street West, in the morning to audition, and then at some point that afternoon, Edie called to say, "You have the third lead in Caligula. The character's entitled Scipio. However, the problem is that you won't be able to do both The Fifth Column," which was the play by Hemingway, "and Caligula. What do you want to do?"

My head was swimming. "When do I have to choose?"

She said, "I can stall them until tomorrow."

"I need to think," I said.

She said, "Sleep on it, and then call me tomorrow."

I went out for drinks with Richard that night, after rehearsal, and Richard said he could tell something was wrong by my mood. He looked at me and said, "What's wrong?"

I told him that I had pursued the audition and so forth, and was offered the role, but that I can't do both.

Without a moments hesitation, he said, "You must do the play."

"It's not that simple. I'm contracted to do this television play," I said.

"Not to worry."

"Oh, yes," I said, "Look, I have no first-hand knowledge of how John Frankenheimer and Sidney behave, or if they're friends, and I have a feeling they are not. I have no real knowledge of the association or relationship, so it may be a little difficult."

"Do you wanna do this play? Aside from it being your Broadway debut in a prestigious work by a great writer, Albert Camus."

"Yes," I said, "and I'm scared as hell."

"Welcome," came this retort immediately, "I'll take care of it," said Richard.

And the next morning, John Frankenheimer came into my dressing room at the TV studio. He looked at me and said, "What's this I hear, you wanna do a play?" he asked.

I said, "Yes, but I don't want to offend you."

He said, "No offense taken, Camus is a great writer. What's the role?"

"Scipio the poet," I said.

"Good casting," he said, "do it, and good luck," he turned around and left the room.

Richard came in and said, "See, I told ya. So, listen, stop by when you can for drinks after your rehearsal, and—".

I looked at him and the rush of everything just flooded in, and I blurted out, "Ya know, I don't know how to thank you."

He said, "the only way you can thank me, is be the very best that you can be."

I Digress

I digress to say so many things in my early life hadn't prepared me in any way to handle the situations I was to encounter in people and society in general. I always had to remind myself of the boy with his nose pressed against the plate window looking at the display of exquisite gems of every description and color, sparkling and refracting the sun's rays, illuminating the unique quality and shape of each of the gems, life in microcosm and a metaphor, I should say.

The flood of people and situations I had only heard of before, or dreamt about, or been in association, occasionally, at the movies, there is an arrogance in not knowing reality as opposed to fantasy. I was more often living in a state of fantasy than living in reality—dreams and nightmares, frankly.

Caligula

The first read-through went rather well, given the extraordinary cast; Colleen Dewhurst was Caesonia, Kenneth Haigh, the English actor who first played Look Back In Anger, with whom I had most of my scenes, would take place, and Sorrell Booke played one of the senators, he did a TV thing, The Dukes of Hazzard.

Love between males in ancient times did not necessarily fall under the heading of homosexuality, as we think of it today. Older Roman males, and Greek males, took the education of the younger men under their wings, and since I'm not qualified to address the historic and conventional manners of those relationships, suffice to say, it was a love relationship, possibly sexual and maybe not.

I took the view that there had been some such feeling of love by Scipio for Caligula, not fully reciprocated by Caligula, given his enigmatic nature, his rather kaleidoscopic history. In the play, Caligula murders Scipio's parents for trivial reasons, and later, in effect, says to Scipio, "do you love me now?" and the first act ends with Scipio embracing Caligula, causing quite a sensation at that time. This was in the early sixties, and for all its joie de vivre, publicly viewed as unacceptable, shocking, if you will.

Sidney did a masterful job of directing this spectacle, replete with every bodybuilder in New York City playing Caligula's praetorian guards. I remember these bodybuilders, and they were always eating something, while in the play there was this huge kind of ham hock, or chicken, or turkey leg, and during one of the scenes I noticed a hand reaching out and grabbing the drumstick of this turkey, and all of a sudden it disappeared.

Needless to say, I was infuriated at the sight of that, and I knew what was going on because I could see peripheral vision, and I never would have believed that somebody would do that because it destroys the reality of the scene and the previous scene, making it no more than a trip to Canter's Delicatessen. Remember, I had just been admitted to the Valhalla of acting world, The Actors Studio, where realism was taken to heights of glory. I played this scene, with Kenneth as Caligula, with all the searing and emotional sweep that erupted like a pent-up volcano. I played it with such force and conviction that Kenneth ripped the upper part of my chiton, which is the robe, what they wore, causing a loud gasp from the audience, which was just exactly what I wanted. I wanted them to be shocked, to shock an audience into paying visceral attention to the horror of Caligula's reign of terror.

Scuttlebutt

Well, the scuttlebutt the next day was, "Well, of course he has to be a homosexual, because otherwise he couldn't play it like that." Then and there the mist of suspicion hung over me for years, the ubiquitous "they" had never heard of substitution, superimposing one behavior for another.

Everybody, it seems, has two professions, their day job and critics of the works at hand of all art in all the fields of entertainment and their audition.

The rehearsal period was intense and everyone was working their way through the text. After all, it was by one of the century's great writers of the absurd. Albert Camus, we were told, would be coming to New York for the opening of the play, and the translation was by a man by the name of Justin O'Brien, a great scholar and a text considered a masterful translation, true to the original text, and the French, as could be had.

If memory serves me correctly, it was a grueling period of rehearsals, all the more so since it was definite that Camus was coming to New York, specifically to attend the opening night. Life Magazine came to the dress rehearsal and started taking pictures to be used in the coming addition of Life Magazine, excitement surrounded the whole affair.

Camus Dead

Two days before the opening night, the producers and Sidney called the cast to get together to give us the devastating news: Camus had been killed in a car accident the day before the dress rehearsal. He was a passenger in the automobile that Gadamer, his publisher, was driving. They were out for a drive and, it seems that, Gadamer drove right into a tree on a country road. Camus was killed instantly and Gadamer was injured badly: an absurd death for a celebrated absurd writer.

We were devastated. I think we vowed to make the opening night a celebration of sorts, a celebrated event of what we believe was a great play in the theatre, and the writing, I still believe that. We ran something like nine weeks and then closed.

Opening Night Party

Opening night parties are tradition in the theatre, and Gloria Vanderbilt, who was then married to Sidney, threw a party to end all parties. It was a snowy evening, opening night, and New York looked as only New York could look in such weather, very much like a child, making it hard to describe.

Gloria and Sidney's apartment occupied what seemed like the penthouse of an enormous apartment building, that bordered on the East River, next to Gracie Park; the Mayor's mansion was just a few blocks away, both off East End Avenue. An elevator took us directly up to the penthouse, only reserved for this particular penthouse, and I remember stepping out of the elevator and being greeted by a maid who took my coat and hung it on a rack with all the others in the foyer. It could have served as a studio apartment, the walls were huge, the room was huge, and that was just the entrance way.

I was then ushered into this enormous living room, beautifully appointed with red cloth paneled walls and crystal chandeliers. As I stepped into the opening room, it seemed as if I had stepped into a Venetian palace. The first thing to catch my eye, was the plethora of peonies, every color and hue, pink, white, red, burgundy, you name it, it was there in huge bunches and it seemed wall-to-wall peonies. She must have spent a fortune in flowers; the rooms were filled with the crème de la crème of all New York intelligentsia and society, the movies and players of every field in artistic endeavor.

The '60's was a very unique time for all of us, some who recognized it for what it was, and some who may have simply looked, bathed into the essence of the time. If the truth were known, I'm always ill at ease with such company, and partly because I had yet to accomplish what I wanted to do and be.

Strange, strange how people change in the surroundings

that they occupy. Does the room change them, the people, the event? I don't know. I haven't a clue, but for me, they do. The stage of a theatre has about as many fields—a Greek Drama, a ParaStyle, a Roman Forum, a private bedroom, a forum of judges. For every play, something uniquely happens and you transform yourself beyond the you that you see in the mirror, the one you ostensibly identify with, the one you're more comfortable with. Is it the true you? I'm never sure.

Hungry for Compliments

As I move through the crowd, hungry for compliments, praise for the work just performed, I did find it. I found it and it was heady in the extreme. As most intelligent people know, you have only one time to make a first impression. Some people decide instantly what will be your fate in the theatre, or any form of entertainment, and indeed in life, as an artist. The energy that pours out of you is, in varying degrees, certain strengths.

I would like to say at this point, you can never really be sure of the subliminal dialog that runs through people's minds. Talk about multitasking, it is nothing short of miraculous, the many dialogs that the mind conducts in the midst of any given conversation. How did all this happen? How did all this come about? A battle of wills ensues, compromises made, and a certain kind of peacefulness is accepted.

Collaborative Work

It's easy to make enemies in any collaborative work, ideas collide, and you learn that the director, in most cases, holds sway, yet the story of any one character is his or her story. Such as "the doctor" in A Streetcar Named Desire is essentially the way the actor is playing the doctor, it's all about the doctor, all about the characters that the doctor comes across. Blanche is only, to the doctor's mind, superfluous, incidental to the doctor's story. You can see what trouble can come for the director; the ones who get away with that kind of thinking are the stars, everything revolves around the stars.

Raise your head above the level and you can get your head handed to you. I'm reminded of an incident in The Aspern Papers, which I will discuss in detail later on.

One has to be careful about the second night after the opening, energy may be down and you mustn't let that happen. I came in the stage door one night, and I was asked to go into Kenneth's room, Kenneth being the Kenneth who played Caligula. I stopped by his room after the play. It seems in the English theatre, it's a sign of respect to make a visit, however brief, to say something, mostly complimentary, to the star of the play. One makes friends that way, and to keep the show running smoothly.

Kenneth Haigh was Caligula, and he was brilliant, I thought that he knew that, but you live and you learn that all of us are supremely insecure. I, more often than might anyone else, felt I could be intruding on their privacy and they would prefer to be left alone. Evidently, in this instance, I was wrong.

Nine weeks just flew by, and the thrill of going to the theatre was a constant thrill. To me, it meant another chance to come close to what I had in my minds eye. Often I would dream about a certain section of the play and how it should be played. I was always at work, even in sleep, and that, of course, could be maddening to the other actors, because I was changing constantly.

A Play Is a Living Thing

To me, a play is a living thing, never set, but always within the realm of the rehearsed outcome. After nine weeks we closed, it was an extraordinary experience, strange events happened in the course of the run. It came about by conversation with Frederick Tozere, who was one of the actors playing the senator. We were having a conversation about the theatre, and in particular, the way one was billed on the marquee in any given Broadway play. He said to me, "If you are billed as a star, you will always be billed as a star, and if you were billed as, let's say featuring, or also starring on the position below the title, then you would also be in that 'also starring' category. You're invariably billed below the title," and he proved to be correct—except in the case of 1776.

Singing Teachers

The musical I had been studying and singing, 1776, I went from one teacher to another, all of whom purported to be singing teachers, but nothing could be further from the truth, until Stephanie Schoolby came into the picture. It is far more difficult to teach a singer who has been badly trained than a new student who has never studied singing. I was of the former, and because people found my voice beautiful, I got away with murder.

I had a very minimal amount of technique. If memory serves me correctly, I started singing as a boy soprano, and I sang with such ease, that soon a couple of scouts from Hollywood had heard about me and came to Toledo to hear this eleven-year-old boy soprano. They came to my house one day, and asked my parents, and particularly my mother, if she would sign a contract for me to go to Hollywood. My brother Alex said that he wanted me to study acting with Mario Spinskia, as he felt I was a natural-born actor. Mostly, my mother said "No." My father was born in Lebanon and really didn't care to speak English that well—he thought it a rather ugly language—so my mother did all the talking.

The guy couldn't believe his ears; "No" to Hollywood—was she crazy? Fame and fortune lay at my feet, according to him, but she would have none of it. Besides, next week I was to sing "Ave Maria" at an orphanage in Momi, Ohio.

It sounds more like the Marx Brothers, a complete non sequitur, "Sing 'Ave Maria' for the orphans," sounds like a real grade-B movie, this angelic boy soprano who could sing one high-C after another, and in one particular instance an E-flat above high-C, phenomenal.

Everyone has heard of the change in a voice that occurs at a certain age in a boy's life. Well, it started to change at age thirteen— high-C's no longer came easily, nevermind E-flat above high-C. The quest for a flawless voice, seamless up and down the scale, was hard to come by. As it happened, some level of these came after a few years of studying with Ms. Schoolby, but I get ahead of myself.

Intense Acting Work

The play closed, and a period of intense acting work commenced with Lee Strasberg at The Actors Studio. Scenes were drawn from every kind of novel. For example, "A Good Man Is Hard To Find," Flannery O'Connor's marvelous short story has a scene of a rather macabre quality; a bible salesman who seduces a farm girl, who happens to have a false leg, and he gets her to take it off, and instead of making love to her, he absconds with her wooden leg, leaving her helpless. And that was some scene, let me tell you.

Then Hamlet came next, the closet scene with the mother Gertrude; besides berating her for her marriage to Claudius, his father's brother, he, in the ensuing scene, happens to kill Polonius, thinking it's Claudius behind an arras, draperies that hung in the room. Polonius just happens to be hiding there behind this tapestry, to test what he feels is Hamlet's madness. As you know, Polonius is Ophelia's father. Hamlet, to my mind, has a sexual relationship with Ophelia and eventually discards her; she's not of royal blood and therefore not material for the role of marriage, Laertes has warned her of that, but to no avail, and—you know the rest of this story.

During this period, I was still living at 451 West 46th Street as a Super, mopping up the hallways, taking out the garbage, all the time working on scenes at The Actors Studio and auditioning for new works, both on and off Broadway.

My Voice

My voice was not the typical Broadway voice, it was somewhere between opera and Broadway, and every audition was a nightmare for me. I had several voice lessons with Stephanie Schoolby every week, so at least my voice was reasonably flexible, the sound could be beautiful. But to my mind, I have never really understood how a voice should function, and consequently, its true potential had never been reached—thanks to so many charlatan maestros.

I now understand what makes a voice both thrilling and easy to produce; high notes not as an armageddon. The craziness that so often accompanies the quest for fabulous technique was always at the back of my mind. The quality of a voice is a unique phenomenon.

When Caruso flogs that "rosa gala," sings, you know immediately who it is. That is what great singing is, no guessing, and that's something that can't be taught, no matter how many years of studying and back-breaking vocalizing one does, it may have something to do with the quality of the vocal chords itself and genetics.

We continued developing as an actor, on various scenes from plays and novels, Shakespeare more often than not. One day Edie called to say that Joe Papp was directing a production of Hamlet for the Shakespeare in the Park Theatre, the one in Central Park, and what a beautiful theatre it was. I auditioned, and Joe Papp offered me the role of Laertes immediately.

Hamlet, or Laertes?

Needless to say, I was thrilled, Joe had assembled a great cast; Alfred Ryder as Hamlet, Howard Da Silva as Claudius, Nan Martin as Gertrude, and Julie Harris as Ophelia. It so happened that Alfred became sick after the opening night, and Bob Behr took over the role of Hamlet. But before that I had gone to Joe and asked him if he would let me play Hamlet.

He said, "I can't, I'll never find a Laertes like you."

I told him I had worked on the role as Hamlet in The Actors Studio, and Laertes was merely the other side of the coin to Hamlet—but I said this to no avail, it was a no-go. I was determined to make my Laertes a complete composite of both roles, and so opening night I pulled out all the stops, and I leapt from about a twelve-foot parapet down to the center-stage in a scene with Claudius. The reviews came out the next day, and one important reviewer said something to the effect of, "Clifford David had all the grace and classical demeanor to play Hamlet," that I should've played Hamlet. Talk about winning the battle and losing the war, this was it. Joe found it hard to forgive me, and I had a difficult time remaining at the Shakespeare festival. I was not a good little boy, willing to subdue my performance in fear of what I knew were the possibilities of a Laertes, and let the other actors bring to bear their full powers to this role, to any role. It's like playing tennis; you always want to play with someone better than you are. So, I tried to be the best that I could, hoping to be matched by anyone on the stage. Some did, and some didn't.

It didn't make any difference, I wasn't there to judge, I was there to work, that's all that mattered to me. I wasn't there to make friends; I was there to be a journeyman actor, doing the job I was hired to do.

Richard Burton and Elizabeth Taylor

I remember one night we held the curtain for Richard Burton and Elizabeth Taylor for the fifth act because, you see, Richard was playing Hamlet on Broadway and we were playing Hamlet in the Central Park, and a big to-do was made about the Burtons coming, Richard Burton and Elizabeth Taylor, coming to the park to see our Hamlet. Limousines were driven in as close to the theatre as possible, police cars escorted them into the park, and the audience was all in a tizzy: Richard Burton and Elizabeth Taylor coming to Central Park to see us.

The papers, the next day, had a golden opportunity for publicity, because Richard sent me a telegram that read, "Receive my offered love, like love, and know that you will not wrong it. Love, Richard." It hangs framed in my library today, along with photos of Marilyn Monroe, given to me by her while we were rehearsing an adaptation of Colette's Chéri. Arthur Miller had made it into a play for Marilyn, specifically, and for me.

The little visit by Richard and Elizabeth created a marvelous and thrilling surprise for the audience, and it took a half an hour for people to gain composure. The fifth act was unlike any fifth act of Hamlet anywhere. The high was just enormous, every actor was in top form, and later we joined Richard and Elizabeth for drinks and an assessment of the play. In short, it was a thrilling evening.

Richard, of course, was one of the great actors in the theatre, and was also a great raconteur of theatre memorabilia.

Roles Against Type

I know I had a great deal to learn, and I set about using The Actors Studio as a venue for experimentation in roles I could be cast in, and many that were against type. Typecasting is basically the major way in which people are cast in plays. I always thought it was talent, but I'm somehow convinced that it was type. At one point I decided to work on Caligula.

There is a huge opening scene in which Caligula taunts Scipio and lays out the gruesome manner in which he murders Scipio's parents, taking the relationship to an absurd level, causing enormous problems. I asked a wonderful studio actor, Lou Antonio, to play Scipio to my Caligula and he consented.

I designed the set in a very simple yet, I thought, striking fashion. The Actors Studio is a rather large church-like form of architecture, huge and open space, exposed ceiling with beams exposed from one side of the building to the other. I found a huge roll of red cloth, so I rolled out black wooden platforms so that they became a raised stage above the three-sided space for the studio members to sit. I then took, what I seemed to remember, as a sort of huge swath of blood-red cloth material and draped it over the main crossbeams in the studio, and I went from one side of the acting space to the other. Then, I took the end of the material and spread it out on the stage, as if blood were spilling all over it. I then lit it from the front and the back so that the color flooded the stage and the actors, bathing everything in blood red, a chiaroscuro effect was achieved. We played the scene to its horrific conclusion of the first act. It's difficult to relate or assess the outcome, but I dare say it stunned everyone, Lee included. One must remember that that period in history was bloody, outrageous in behavior, completely passionate on every level, and it's safe to say the performance was hugely successful. I think every actor in the place wanted to try their hand at it. Paul Newman came up to me and was extraordinarily generous in his compliments.

Marilyn Monroe and Arthur Miller were there that day, as were Maureen Stapleton, Jerry Page, and a whole host of everybody you could possibly know from the movies or the theatre. The Actors Studio was packed with truly gifted actors.

It was, I dare say, successful, given what happened shortly after the session. Lee asked me to stop by his office afterwards. No matter what others may have thought of him, he was one of the preeminent acting teachers in the world. I owe much of my career to his help and opening many doors for me. There was a rush of energy and high-wire emotions that coursed through my veins and body after such a session, and there were many different-sided feelings. I played it full-out in the classical fashion, and I'm not sure that others cared to be on the same stage, maybe feeling overwhelmed, but I held nothing back, and that's just my personal feeling about it.

I went downstairs to Lee's office, I walked in and he was writing something at his desk. He looked up and said, "Oh, Clifford, could you come to my apartment this afternoon?"

I was rather nonplussed, but I said, "Sure, what time?"

"Well, sometime after you've had your lunch."

I said, "Okay."

"Good, I'll see you there," and he returned to his writing.

I walked out and thought what did he want of me, never dreaming of what actually would take place. I was too nervous to eat, so I just had coffee. That's what I need, a piece of bread. My stomach was turning, and my stomach has always been supersensitive, no more so than ever. What could he want? I had no idea, and I wondered if it had anything to do with the scene. Did he think highly of it? He said he did during the critique.

Was he disappointed in the work? The insecurities just rushed in, and, given the end of the scene was raunchy and brutal in the extreme, and any human relationship that you can remember, that takes place between two men—not much is left to the imagination. I don't mean to imply that it was obscene, but it was heady to say the least.

Two-thirty approached as I walked into his apartment on Central Park West, and I remember books lined the entire hallway, photographs of everybody in the theatre and movies, Eleanora Duse, Salvini, Stanislavski, et cetera. It was very impressive to say the least.

Paula Miller, who was Mrs. Strasberg at that time, greeted me at the door, and said, "He's waiting for you in the library, down the hall," and with that said, she turned and left. Okay, down the hall.

The door was closed, so I knocked, and I heard Lee's voice say, "Come in." I opened the door, and I think my mouth dropped to the floor. Lee was sitting there with Marilyn Monroe and Arthur Miller.

Lee said, "sit down Clifford." Well, I didn't nearly sit down, I nearly fell down. Now, one has to remember, contextually, that this is a kid from Toledo, Ohio, and so much had happened in the few years in New York City, that most of it seemed like a dream, and now Marilyn Monroe and Arthur Miller and Lee Strasberg, and I was in the same room with them.

About Marilyn

What has been written about Marilyn Monroe has been different for every person who has come into contact with her. It runs the gamut of descriptions, I found constant change in her personality given whatever circumstances she felt was required of her. It was from the little girl to the complete woman in charge of everything. One must remember that she physically changed by gradations from Norma Jean Baker into Marilyn Monroe. Her idea of what a movie star should look like and whatever went on in her mind was impossible to describe.

The complete awareness of what was taking place at whatever every moment was happening it swept you up without your ever hardly be aware that. As far as I was concerned in my own mind it was hard to believe that she was taken advantage of by every male who ever came into her life.

Enigma is a pale word to describe the reality of her inner life; when Marilyn came out of her room something had changed in her, it seems to be a true transformation that had taken place. A light went off in my head, so to speak, that her idea—that is Marilyn's idea of the character of Leah, of the woman of the world and my character's name was "Sherry." Nothing could be more to the point than the true differences in each of us—Marilyn as "Leah" had personal experiences in her life that far exceeded anything that happened in my life and the world knew you, really you, surpassed anything to the imagination. I have always had the image of a jeune premier, that is a boyish quality no matter what age I truly was. A kind of boy/man naïf, if you will, and since Lee had recommended me to Arthur and Marilyn, he knew better than anyone, particularly after I had three intensive years of studying with him. It dawned on me that it was perfect type casting. Typecasting to perfection.

Cheri is to be taught the ways of the world by Leah and who better than Marilyn to teach it to Clifford. I have to be careful to hold at bay anything I thought I knew and be open to be taught by all that Marilyn knew, all her experiences in life that I could only guess at. A boy with a woman and I never fully realized just how young I was in comparison with what Marilyn Monroe knew.

This iconic star had come into contact with all the bigwigs in the movie industry. Barracudas all and in fact "killers"! They didn't run studios on their looks and personalities. The directors held all the power of the completed movie. And she had crossed swords with them all and ultimately won over her vision for the characters she plays at her basic native instinct. It seems the world at large may have had the image of her as a dumb blonde, nothing could be further from the truth.

Marilyn Monroe was very smart in the ways that count in managing her career. Just look at the monumental effort she exhibited in changing her complete physical person from a little better than ordinary-looking girl, and the change into a sex symbol to end all sex symbols. Again iconic is the only word for her transformation from Norma Jean Baker into the goddess Marilyn Monroe.

The Cat

The difficulty in describing the emotional state, given what I had just done by performing in Caligula at The Actors Studio with everyone packed to the gills, it was too much to digest and truly comprehend at that time. I sat down, hardly before falling down, and they, Marilyn and Arthur, congratulated me on the work, and I got out a "thank you."

Lee said, "Arthur has begun to work on a translation of a novel by Colette called The Cat, and he's turning it into a two-character play for Marilyn, and they would like you to play the young man."

Well, you can imagine, it was like somebody hit me in the head with a frying pan, I was speechless.

"Would you like to do that?" he said.

I looked at him and said, "Yes, most certainly."

I barely got out the sentence when he said, "Good. Marilyn will call you on Monday with the beginning time for rehearsal, and she'll tell you where. Arthur has a few scenes that you could start working on."

He looked at me and kind of smiled and said, "Okay, that'll be all."

Well, I was glad that was all because I couldn't take much more, I was in the same room with one of the great icons of the Twentieth Century in the movies, and also one of the truly great playwrights of all time. Was I dreaming? Could this be happening to me?

I walked out of the apartment facing Central Park West and took a deep breath, as much as I possibly could inhale, my head became lightheaded and that incredible bubble of joy erupted instantly. My body, that giggle of life, the phrase I am about to write is one that I am sure other actors may have quoted Marilyn as saying, but I swear it happened to me.

On that Monday morning, just as Lee said she would,

she called while I was having my morning coffee. When the phone rang I jumped, was shaken rather frankly and half in a daze, I picked up the phone and I said, "Hello?"

This lovely, soft, voice was on the line, and I kept asking myself, "Is it Marilyn? Is this Marilyn?" Well of course it was Marilyn.

She said, "Hello, Clifford, this is Marilyn Monroe from class." Well, whom else could it be with that voice, it sounded unbelievably like Sugar in "Some Like It Hot."

"This is Marilyn from class." The rest of the conversation has become sort of dreamlike, a fog, if you will, in which one merely feels one's way through it. It ended with, "I'll pick you up in a car. Where do you live?"

Frankly, I didn't want the neighborhood to see me get into whatever kind of car would be arriving at my door, and I'm sure it would be a limousine. So I said, "Look, I'd rather meet you on 9th Avenue and 50th Street," or 46th Street, I can't quite remember, "and next time, would it be alright if I just walk to your place?"

She said, "No, it's not necessary, I need to do some things."

"Sure," I said, "Okay."

"Can I have the driver come to your door?"

"No, no," I said, "You can just drop me off at the corner, I have to take my laundry there."

"Well, okay," came this soft, cotton candy voice. My God, I've got to get out of that place, because 9th and 10th Avenue could be a little rough, Hell's Kitchen was what it was called, and that's a very apt name. It was also appropriate for the district and for my neighborhood, nice people, but it was a rough neighborhood. I didn't want them to see me get into this limousine, and then they would try to guess who was in the car, or the vehicle, or the limousine, whatever it may be.

Sure enough, a long limousine pulled up in front of me, and on the northwest side of 9th Avenue the doors opened and the driver got out, opened the door for me.

I got in, and there was Marilyn in a kind of summer dress and a babushka-like over her head and dark sunglasses. For me, it was like all the air got sucked out of the backseat. I was enclosed in the soft, very comfortable seats and the faint, but very faint aroma of perfume, delicate. She said, "Do you mind if we stop first at Saks Fifth Avenue? I want to pick up some things to take to the country this weekend."

The country being the home that they had bought, or rented, I'm not sure which, in Amagansett, on the island, Long Island, that is.

"No, whatever you want," I said. Damn right, whatever you want. We got out of the limo on the 50th Street side and we went into Saks, right into a waiting elevator, obviously they knew she was coming. What happened next could've come out of a NewBridge movie, every shot was perfection. We were whisked up to whatever floor it was, 6th maybe, and we were greeted by a sales lady. She greeted us very warmly, not in any way subservient, but definitely aware of who she was attending to, along with me.

We walked to a remote section on the floor that displayed row after row of hats, scarves, and various high-end boutique stuff. Someone brought out two pink velvet-covered chairs and motioned for us to sit. The sales lady said to Marilyn, "I'm so glad you could stop by today, as we just received a great variety of new hats by so many of the new designers." I was witness to a kind of Florenz Ziegfeld being of a tall model coming in wearing every imaginable ensemble and shape of hat, a lot of them with huge brims and all kinds of flowers on them, every shade of pastel, every shade of white you could imagine, and they were on these gorgeous models, and Marilyn was so sweet with them. I'm sure that she knew and felt that, in some manner or other, she had been there, she knew what that was about, selling something or other.

On display at every turn, she kindly said to the sales lady, "May I try a few of them on?"

"Of course Miss Monroe," and she motioned for the girls to come forward and take off their hats, and the sales lady then handed them to Marilyn to try on. Well, I think you get the picture. It was as if the room was flooded with pale pink, and the vision of beauty radiated throughout, and the breathtaking extent of her being, even to the floors we haven't been on, I know I exaggerate, but just picture Florenz Ziegfeld directing a bevy of beauties offering these incredible hats to the goddess of the screen, who tried them on one after another, and the shade of pink changed to whatever color she was wearing, it would be pink, it would be gray, it would be yellow, it would be all colors of the very palest of pastels of the highest quality. She was trying on every hat in the place, and I could've only dreamed of such another world, l'après-midi d'un faune sort of atmosphere (The Afternoon of a Faun).

With mist covering practically everything, nothing seemed to be totally clear, it was just as if there was a haze, a beautiful kind of velvet kind of haze, covering everything, particularly her, it was like it was a dream.

Marilyn finally bought a total of twenty-six hats. Well, there must have been no hats in Amagansett at all anymore. Twenty-six hats? How are you going to wear them all?

She asked very kindly if they could be delivered to the house in Amagansett, and of course the sales lady said, "Absolutely, it'll be there this weekend for you."

Marilyn, very graciously, thanked all the models and the sales lady, and I thought to myself, "How the hell am I gonna rehearse after this dreamlike affair? Where's reality?" the overall view of everyday life was kind of faded somewhere in the background.

Somehow I managed to follow Marilyn out of the store, into a waiting limousine, and ushered away as fast as we could down East 57th Street to a very new apartment. It was a beautiful apartment, from what I remember, very high up on the highest floors, and probably one of the most elegant buildings in all of New York City.

Once we got into this private elevator going up to what seemed to be the penthouse, the first thing I noticed in the living room, in a rather large living room, was a huge white grand piano. It was white, and I hadn't seen a white piano except in the movies. The room was beautifully appointed, comfortable chairs, every shape and size, covered in chintz fabric. It had the immediate quality of being like a country retreat; it was absolutely beautiful and colorful and one that you would expect to see in one of the most elegant of houses, or apartments, in New York City.

Marilyn said to me, "Make yourself comfortable and I'll be back shortly." Well, shortly turned out to be about forty-five minutes or so.

Later she came out and she said, "I'm so sorry I took so long, but"—and this is really rather kind of important, I was just shaken, in a way, because next she said—"I'm so sorry it took so long, but I had to be sure just who would come out, and I had to really know that I was that person coming out of the bathroom, and I had to be ready to rehearse."

It turned out that she was in her bedroom lavatory, and I'm sure she was studying her image to be sure it managed to conform to the image she wished to portray, and also the image that she thought was typical of Colette's Chéri. And I will say, she had changed the whole aura of her whole person—it was transformative, to say the least.

She had a full-blown idea of what she wanted from this character and this work, and consequently just who Chéri was, and in my opinion, fairly close to what Colette had written about Chéri.

We rehearsed one of the scenes that Arthur had worked on, and almost two hours, later we decided that that was enough for today and she offered the car to me to take me home.

I said, "No, no, thank you. But since I'm so close to

Bloomingdale's I'll just go there and walk home, but thank you very much for the offer."

My character had a very sensual air about him, much like Aaron Deumot, and possibly diffident at the same time, rather withdrawn, and yet this kind of atmosphere of mystery about this particular character that Colette had drawn. I tried to manage to meld myself with and become that person. It gave me a slight mysterious quality, but also very, very engaging. The audience mustn't be too sure at first how this character would develop. I brought up all the sense-memory that I could call upon, my fingertips waiting to explore the entire hidden situation. When I got home I laid down, and I daydreamed for quite some time before I realized that it was dark outside. Many of the challenges that a character presents, I often find a hint of a solution, and sometimes something of a full-blown solution to what was needed to accomplish the life of the character and myself.

It's when I am relaxed and not forcing an idea toward a conclusion that I'm more open to receive images and ideas that lead to more creative solutions, and often unconventional ones, and the result was unconventional, but believable.

Actors often stand in their own way and accept a less inspired result. We see this so often, in my opinion, in the works presented to the public by so many actors of extraordinary talent, but it never really comes to fruition.

The colder the personality in acting is a dead-end, however it can be in vain of recognizable brand, which is not all together bad, just limiting, celebrity acting, limiting, not inventive, just more of the same color, actors who seem to play the same role in every character they play. Perhaps in a different shade of blue, but still, it was blue.

Several days passed before I heard from Marilyn as to the next time we would rehearse, and when she called this time, it was just, "Hi, Clifford, it's Marilyn."

"Hi," I answered.

"Could we rehearse tomorrow?" she said.

"Of course," I said, "I'll just leave it up to you. Whenever you wish to rehearse," I said, "I'll be there," I tried to be not deferential, but honest.

"Good," she said, "I'll pick you up on the same side of the street as before. Is two o'clock good for you?"

I said, "Sure, I'll be ready."

"Great, I'll see you at two o'clock, as usual, at the corner of 9th Avenue. Oh, and by the way, for now," she said, "the limo will pick you up maybe a little bit before two, so if you could be there just a bit before."

Well, true to her word, the limo was a little early to pick me up, and there was Marilyn sitting in the backseat. Every encounter with her seemed half like a dream. I mean, remember, I'm dealing with an icon, someone that you've seen on the screen seventy feet high.

I had to get rid of the idea of, or the sense of, awe, so that I could get down to work. The work at hand was hard, and as Colette is so specific in her delineation of characters, one has to be very careful not to overdo, but to be the essence of what she was after.

In order to receive a result close to the scene at hand, all the work between actors, each has to make sure that the quality of the work in no way differs from the star status, and this can be difficult.

It is a difficult task to achieve, as I will recount episodes from a play entitled Aspern Papers by Henry James, work adapted by Sir Michael Redgrave, whereas some stars who take this attitude as a threat to the august supremacy.

My attitude has always been "to hell with that, the work is all," not a very enduring quality, never rude or mean, but just a respect for every actor, not matter what the marquee value was, every mosaic of the whole is vital to the success of any work. This philosophy may be difficult for some people to swallow, but the use of the ego is vital. Yet not an ego that damages relationships with everyone at hand. Anything less than one's very best is a disservice to the author, to your fellow actors, and to the audience.

Ego and energy require constant monitoring, not too much, but just enough to accomplish the end result. And how do you accomplish this? Particularly with this icon sitting next to me, or working across from me, the darling of the public at large, and in fact, in the entire world, was witnessed that even today her name and visions are still everywhere and revered throughout the world.

The Lawsuit

Then we came to what seemed to be a rather abrupt end, because Marilyn had been in, as I understood it, a contentious lawsuit with Twentieth Century Fox. She, for whatever reason, did not want to continue working with Twentieth Century Fox or the projects that they were supposed to have already built her in. It went to court and, ultimately, she lost the lawsuit and was forced to go back to Hollywood to finish a picture, a movie that she did not want to do.

She was very sweet, very warm, and very sincere, and she apologized, but she said, "I'm coming back, don't worry we'll work on it because I love this play and I love working with you," and then she said, "I want you to have this picture," and she gave me a picture which I have never seen anywhere else in any of the books, it was a very special picture.

I believe it was taken by Herb Greene, I'm not sure if that's true, but it was a picture I have never seen anywhere. Anyway, she gave it to me, there was no autograph on it, and the picture was of her in bed covered in a silk kind of coverlet holding a rose. She didn't sign it, and it was her very subtle sign of respect for a fellow actor, and I quote her here, she said, "I know you, and you don't need me to sign it for you. You know who I am, what we worked on and you don't need me to sign it." It was very sweet of her and it was, in a way, very respectful.

There has, I suspect, always been a rather shy demeanor about her, and a feeling I had that she felt deferential to people, such as myself, who have already been on Broadway, and that theatre actors held a very special place for her.

She had a deep desire, a hunger, to learn, and wanted to be considered a great actress, no matter that she was already an icon of the world, and not just a sexual icon, but certainly she worked on herself in a way that made her extraordinarily beautiful. She was such a Hollywood success in the extreme, there are very few that have garnered that kind of niche in the world of movies.

More Rehearsal

But, I'm getting ahead of myself, back to the limo we go.

On the way to rehearsal at her apartment, she turned to me and said, "Would you mind if, on the way, we stopped by this place that sells material and wallpaper?" Well, this place that she was referring to, sells not only material and wallpaper, but it's one of the premiere houses of art decorators of houses and such, and they're just top of the line, a place that exhibited probably some of the most beautiful material and the latest and most current in beautiful design. One of their specialties was wallpaper that matched material in which draperies were to be made.

We stopped on Madison Avenue in the Fifties, got out and, again, went into a waiting elevator—they obviously were expecting her, and it was reserved exclusively for Brunswick and Fee. When we got out of the elevator, a man dressed to the hilt came to greet this vision of beauty, and before he could greet her, she said, "hello, this is Marilyn Monroe, I wonder if you remember me?"—and I don't think was a put on, that "I wonder if you remember me" was actually how she felt. It was not just being polite or, in any way, falsely derogatory, she did mean it, "I wonder if you remember me"—she meant that. I mean, my God, who could forget her.

Anyway, she wanted to pick up some things for the house in Amagansett. I think he was a little shocked, but he composed himself enough to say, "Of course Ms. Monroe. I just put aside some things that I wanted you to see."

"I'm so glad," said Marilyn, and she said, "Oh yes, by the way, this is my actor friend Clifford David." The usual "It's a pleasure," and the usual polite chat ensued, although I'm sure he couldn't care less of who I was. He ushered us into a room with row upon row of materials that just hung, and the wallpaper to match. We sat down, again, in very comfortable chairs, and he brought out truly beautiful material of every design and color.

Strange how things happen—many years later that I was to visit this place, looking with my, then, wife for material and wallpaper for the house that we had in California, my brain was rather in a very different place. How often things happen that you revisit something that you'd done before, it was somehow déjà vu, very different, and yet here we were looking at all this extraordinary and beautiful material, expensive to say the least, and we would eventually find some that we would use in some way.

Marilyn had a great appreciation for beautiful things, and her quest for beauty was never more evident than in her own transformation of her body and face. Look at photos of Norma Jean Baker and then look at the next exposure of time in which she turned herself, transformatively, into Marilyn Monroe—that answers it all.

Now was the time to change that inner being, and it began with choosing Lee Strasberg and The Actors Studio as a starting point. Single-mindedness of purpose, both the icon of the cinema, beauty, and a great actress, if you study. You have to study "Some Like It Hot,"; Marilyn as Sugar is a complete realization of Sugar, as anyone could ever have hoped for, or dreamed of, perfection in every way, down to playing Marilyn Monroe as Sugar. I believe that says it all.

We started work on Chéri, in earnest, and in a way that foretold how her Chéri would come to life. My character was, as I wanted him to, a transfixed man of complete adoration of her, not just sexual, but thrilled to be captivated by her simplicity and complete acceptance of her beauty. One of the images that I had, and still have, of Colette and her writings, is an air of luxurious earthly splendor, one of the complete images that I had taken in the form of, as I imagined it, a long strand of luxurious, lustrous pearls, being dipped into a large and beautiful porcelain cup of dark chocolate, and

then held above an open mouth, which sucked the choco-
late-covered pearls dry. In the mixture of the chocolate and
the pearls as an aphrodisiac of exquisite sense and sensibility,
as in a dream, this vision started very quickly and ended just
as quickly.

Marilyn discussed the lawsuit with Twentieth Century
Fox, it was on her mind, it was over some infraction of a contract, or a dispute, and certain pictures whose material she
didn't like, artistic differences was one way of putting it. She
lost the lawsuit and had to go back to Hollywood, as I said, to
complete a contractual agreement on a film, I believe it was
called Something's Gotta Give, and it did.

Marilyn was done in by it, and several memories come to
mind; the timeframe to them is confusing to me even now, so
I will merely recount them.

At one point in my association with Marilyn I was invited
to the opening of a screening of The Misfits, which Arthur
Miller had written specifically for her, and it starred Clark
Gable, Montgomery Clift, and Marilyn. I remember Eli Wallach played a wonderful character, but I can't remember his
association with Marilyn, and naturally, Clark Gable was the
major love interest. In my mind's-eye, I can see Marilyn on
Arthur Miller's arm as we came out of the screening, facing
the adoring crowd. Next, Marilyn was off to Hollywood, and
our rehearsals were interrupted. She said to me, "As soon as
this picture is finished, I'll be back and we can work on Chéri.
I'm so sorry to stop now, but you see, I've lost my lawsuit."
I said to her, "I'll be ready any time you say. Break a leg"—
that's the theatre talk for wishing the actor the very best, not
good luck, which seems to be bad luck, but much like actors
never mentioning Macbeth, they call it "the Scottish play,"
otherwise, it might bring bad luck. Superstitions, superstitions, superstitions. I had an awful feeling, not only one of
disappointment, but somehow, I was very sad for her. Most
actors would kill to be on their way to Hollywood to star

in a major movie, I think it was with Yves Montand in Let's Make Love, or Dean Martin in Something's Got To Give. It seemed that things were falling apart on every level for her, her marriage to Arthur was in serious trouble, and she had, somewhere along the way, it seems, lost a baby, and everything was rather sad and not good for her, and then one of those Hollywood magazines came out with naming me as Marilyn's last love, just plain garbage and that kind of thing is what I hate most, trash, that only the entertainment industry can dig it up. It seems we had been spotted on our shopping trips by whomever, the paparazzi or someone else, and none of it is true, and then, the next thing I knew, Marilyn was dead, she was found in her house in LA.

Again, oddly enough, many years later when I was married, my wife and I looked at a house in Brentwood; we were interested in it and thinking of buying it, but before the papers were signed, I was told that Marilyn had lived in this house. The agent was careful enough not to say that this was the house that she died in, because that would end of the deal. Not in your life would I have a house in which this extraordinary creature lived and died, it was not a pleasant thought. We already had a beautiful house in   Santa Monica, and this was intended as an investment.

Now, one of Marilyn's dear friends, Ralph Roberts, who was also a friend of mine, was a confidante, a masseur, and a lovely human being. He had saved her, it seems, twice before, I believe, from an overdose, only this last time, he was in New York, she was in Hollywood, in Brentwood actually, in this house. The details may never be known in truth by someone, or anyone, but all kinds of theories abound, none of which I will recount.

Shortly after this awful tragedy, Lee called me and asked me if I would accompany him to see the final rushes of Marilyn in her latest movie. We went to a studio on Broadway, and we were ushered into a screening room, and on the screen, when the cameras started to roll, was one of the most incredible clips of Marilyn I will ever remember.

It was a scene in which she was swimming nude in a blue pool. I mean the water was so blue that it looked like the Sea of Marmara outside Istanbul. Marilyn was tanned in this blue swimming pool, hair bone-white, cut short, and as she swam up to the edge of the pool where we were sitting, you could see it was like we were right next to her, and smiling radiantly, gorgeous was not the word, it was just breathtaking. It is so completely difficult for me to see this image of Marilyn, just juxtapose to the Marilyn I knew from rehearsals, and now I fully realized that she was dead.

As I told you before, at one point during our rehearsals she went into the bathroom and stayed there for fully forty-five minutes, and when she came out she smiled sweetly and said, "I wanted to be sure which Marilyn I wanted you to see." Stunning in its implication and not totally lost on me. Which Marilyn?

Well, I wanted the one who she really was at heart, the one who wanted to be considered a serious actress, and one who would have the possibility, the potential, to be great. My God, she was already, as an actress in movies, extraordinary beyond belief, and, as I said, an icon of incomparable stature. Look around you, and to this day photos of her abound in every medium, she is everywhere.

So many actors, whether they can admit it or not, have patterned themselves after her, they have done so many in every physical possible way to change themselves, she went beyond superstardom, so as to become mythic, in my opinion. I have resisted writing about her for many reasons, and not the least of these is always that sensationalism that is attached to her, she was a human being with all the faults and foibles each of us has, and with it all she, like any true artist, tried to match what each has in his or her mind's eye and bring it to life in the material world, a sacred part of her to be shared, witnessed, and revered. She did it. She did it fully, maybe not all in the way she truly wished to be seen, but she did it for all to see.

Much to Accomplish

I needed to put all of this behind me, and quickly, there is much I have to accomplish, and in truth, much to work on that I found wanting in me and my work and what I had in my mind's eye. After many auditions I landed a major role in a project that starred Lucille Ball entitled Wildcat.

Once again, I came up against a truly unusual woman. Lucy was no ordinary entertainer, she, in my opinion, is probably the greatest comedienne of the Twentieth Century, and maybe for all time, I don't know. First and foremost, Lucy was a theatre person, she was known by very few people as "Two Gun," that was her beginning Broadway experience as a chorus girl, and this comes from a truly great and dear friend of mine who was with her in this show, this Broadway play., Unfortunately, she's since died, that is, Gladys Burch. She was in the chorus on Broadway with Lucy and some musical or other before I was in Wildcat.

Digression: Mannes Music School

I digress to account the early days as a scholarship student at the Mannes Music School. I'm not at all sure how all this came about. Early on in my New York sojourn, I wanted to sing and act, so singing came first, and the study of music from every aspect that could be considered a musical education: piano, composition, and a voice trained with a number of teachers.

At the school I met a lot of aspiring students in every field of endeavor. One of my school friends at The Mannes, who was studying composition and piano, had found a place, through friends, up in East Harlem. It was the top floor of a coldwater house, and he asked me if I would like to share the top floor; we'd each have our own bedroom and a living room with a wood-burning fireplace, which we needed desperately because there was no heat in the house.

He already had a wonderful Steinway Grand, so that went in the living room, and I said, "Of course." The rent was fairly reasonable and I was very lucky, at that point, to find a place to live, so I shared the rent. Like so many things in life, the right thing just happened. The place was at 529 East 118th Street.

The woman who had rented the whole house from two sisters named Nikolai, had to make ends meet, so she rented out the top floor to us, and her name was Gladys Burch. She was a writer, formerly a young woman who had been on Broadway, and who happened to be working on a book of the life of Richard Wagner. She had also been in the chorus on Broadway, and was now writing this particular book that was to be the definitive book on Wagner for Brentano's, which was a big book store. From her I learned of Lucy being called "Two Gun," funny how things fall in to place. I knew Gladys long before Wildcat, and this house was a meeting place of so many fabulously interesting people from all over the world. Gladys was one of the most loving and generous people that I had ever met and would ever meet again. There wasn't a bone in her body that was mean or inconsiderate or ungiving.

It wasn't long before we were in her kitchen eating the food that she so lovingly cooked and worked so hard on. I had some money because I did part-time work and managed to save a few dollars, so I tried to let her know that I would be more than happy to contribute. I did not want to sit at her table and not participate by either giving her money or bringing food to the table so that we could all share it. It was a scene that could be compared to a life of La Bohème of Puccini. My friend Peter Terry, a gifted pianist and composer, and Gladys, a writer, Boris Tetenko, a Russian émigré who visited often, and a beautiful young English lady by the name of Deborah who had psychic abilities about her which she guarded very carefully, not at all like so many who paraded about for some kind of cache or special attention, she was very secretive about it.

Now, when I said a "coldwater house", I mean a cold water house, there was no heat, no hot water, a pot-bellied stove on the upper floor, and the ovens were the source that gave off heat for the house, and it was needed, it was freezing that winter. Winter after winter the windows would just frost up from the cold. The kitchen was on the first floor, and it was very large, a real kind of country kitchen with a huge round table that could seat as many as eight or ten people comfortably, and there a wood-burning fireplace in the kitchen that served as a place in which the cook stuck a pot. She, in particular, was a great cook—numbered among her friends, were Julia Child and Louisette, a French lady with whom Julia Child co-authored a book, which received great acclaim, that also gave as its lineage French cooking as well as American cooking. Gladys could really cook, and in such a generous way, and usually she would cook food that could feed any number of people who may be hungry, and that was usually the case, because she always fed Peter and myself, she fed us and really nurtured us and our aspirations.

Peter had a beautiful Steinway grand that occupied half the living room upstairs and it was a magnificent instrument. Peter generously blocked out time for each of us, he needed to practice his work, and I had time to practice my music. I was learning the piano, playing, and also composition and vocalizing. The Mannes School was a truly great conservatory, and David Mannes was a superb violinist who, so I'm told, studied with the great Ysaÿe. Walter Damrosch was related to the family, I think he was a brother-in-law, and Marya Mannes was a celebrated author. The faculty was absolutely superb and first-rate on every score, in every area, teacher by teacher, many from Germany and France, as well as Americans who had obtained prominence in their fields. Dr. Felix Salzer was a man for composition, and Shirley Van Brunt, for the piano, and Frank Sherman, an extraordinary pianist, taught piano there. He taught so many of the younger up-and-coming pianists. Then, there's Claire Wood who taught voice, she had studied in Paris, and she was a beautiful singer. There are so many others, like Carl Bamberger from Germany who taught conducting, the conservatory had a definite dramatic regime, strict, no nonsense, and you had to know your business and no one graduated unless you were up to snuff. And if you had a career in mind, you had fierce competition in every field to compete with, and compete against. If I learned anything about this discipline, it was at The Mannes Conservatory. I never knew where any of this would leave me. I think my modus operandi was "Let's try this and see what happens, let's see how it goes."

Voice, the Greatest Challenge

I believe that's why so much of my life has been a series of episodic periods of adventures, but after all that is said and done, this quest for greatness was still somewhere to be sought. My voice has always offered the greatest challenge, it has always been quixotic (I'll delve into that later), in the musicals I did on Broadway and everywhere else. Meanwhile, life at Gladys Burch's was filled with people in every walk of life, writers, artists, painters, musicians, from all over the world. Peter's family was an extraordinary diverse group of people who came from a unique background. The family, if I remember correctly, was a part of that fabled group "The New York 400." He never played it up, it was just something that I found out. They were a rather exclusive club, and the family has lineage going back to the Mayflower. Anyway, they never really made any real big deal about it, in the sense as the Rockefeller's did, and they never made any bones about their extraordinary wealth.

The Terry's were not that wealthy, but they were unbelievably well connected to just about everybody in New York society. They were truly a marvelous family, very, very musical. The Terry's, Peter's family, had a house in New Canaan, Connecticut, and many a weekend we were invited to spend there, and great company was brought about. From all over the world people came from every country, and all these various people were incredibly gifted at one thing or another— they were painters, they were writers, they were artists, it was just incredibly stimulating times from every aspect, musical and literary conversations and discussions.

You had to be very much on your toes at the times it seemed like something out of another century. Piano playing, usually Bach, Brahms, or Beethoven, the discussions of literature and philosophy all filled the air. Naturally, people would arrive with groups of friends from New York and Europe. Friday evening, the Terry's house was a warm and beautiful country house, large dinning room, dinner was always lively, and the cook had always prepared some wonderful combination of foods, and the times that the Terry's cooked, it was equally as lovely. But, the important thing was the exchange of intellectual topics, it made my mind spin and wanting all the more to excel in as many directions as possible, no limits to anything.

I saw and experienced a part of New York I never would have known about. Peter's grandmother, Mrs. Trafford, belonged to a club called the Cosmopolitan Club, and believe me, it was as its name, cosmopolitan, it implied that you had to get on your best, or else. Peter was one of five brothers, there was Arthur, Tim, Brad, and James, and they were a great group of guys, each one had very specific qualities about them, and they were good acquaintances, interesting, well-traveled, educated, and the world made smaller, because it seemed that just about everybody in the world came through that house.

Gladys was also a good friend of theirs; later she bought a wonderful old house in New Canaan, and eventually started her own bookstore in Darien, while writing this book on Wagner, it was called Burch Books, across from the train station in Darien. It was really one of those bookstores that had a Dickensian feel about it, that was filled to overflowing with books of every sort and description, and they were usually piled on the floor so that you had to wind your way through a very small aisle, but she knew exactly where every book was. Some were piled high, practically to the ceiling, and some you just had to walk around, and, as I said, make no mistake, Gladys knew where every book was on every subject matter, no matter what. There were many, many first editions, a plethora, a gold mine, as it were, of books.

It was a place for everyone, writers, or anyone who had

any aspirations of being either a writer, a musician, a painter, in every possible field there were books that could talk about the work that was done by others, people of every subject. In many ways it was a difficult, if stimulating, life for her, long hours and then home to continue working on her tome of Wagner. The research was to be as complete as possible, research of his life, his works, and his whole being; it was to be the definitive book on Wagner, anywhere. However, I am sorry to say that she died before it could be finished, but that's another story, and a very sad one, and one I will complete and fill in the future, starting with her being on Broadway with Lucille Ball, although Gladys always referred to her as "Two Gun."

Lucille Ball

Wildcat was a thrilling adventure for me, the book was by N. Richard Nash, a very highly respected and acclaimed writer, and Lucille Ball produced it.

It was a time when I think she was getting divorced from Desi Arnaz, and this was a way for her to use her energies and creativity and constructive work. She worked like a horse practically, day and night figuring out what to do and how to do it, to make something of a book, that had some faults with it, the story itself.

The story is of a woman who's a wildcat oil person; the music was by Cy Coleman, another prolific composer, and wonderful. Michael Kidd did the choreography. Any of you who don't remember or know Michael Kidd, he was one of the most marvelous modern choreographers, fabulous dancer, and he developed into a wonderful director. As choreographer and director, he did the movie Seven Brides For Seven Brothers, and he was known for building things right on the set, and observing everybody in the audience watching, how it was done.

In Wildcat, he built a derrick, and he was just superb to watch, it was real theatricality. They were a legendary group of people, to say the least, and headed by Lucille Ball; she became a legend in her own time, and still is. Wildcat, I believe, started as a project for Lucy to do while in the midst of her divorce with Desi. No matter what anyone says, again, my opinion, she loved him deeply, but could no longer put up with his infidelities.

They, together, formed Desilu, one of the prime inventors of the three-camera technique for Hollywood sitcoms, one that is still in use today. They built an empire, and one that she would later head as an executive, a major executive of a studio. She did it all.

In the beginning, it was Desi who was a master at producing, and together they learned from each other. There are others who know much more about this than I do; it is legendary in the field of entertainment and studio lore and history.

Rehearsals started in Hollywood, at the Masonic Temple on Hollywood Boulevard, and then we moved to New York after the first few days of read-through and the table-read, in which all the actors would sit around and we would read the play, so that we knew where we were as far as dramatic situation was concerned.

You may not know what a read-through really is until you've been in one. You sit around this table, and everybody has a say as to what is and what isn't, and what should be and what needs to be done. Lucille was very open to people's suggestions—and the play needed work. She knew that, but it was a vehicle for her, and the tangential characters in it supported her.

It is also a moment of first impressions. You had to be at your very best, because no matter what occurred, everyone stays in listening intently and making judgments as to the quality of your work, judging every line of the way and making an assessment as to whether the person hired to that role was right for it. There is still, I believe, a five-day period in which an actor can be fired or relieved of his or her role in the work, if they didn't think that you matched up to what they had originally thought that you could deliver—so you better be good.

Just as an audition is, in fact, a performance. Don't let anyone kid you, there is no such thing as an audition, an audition is a chance to perform, and what you think is necessary for the role, what you bring to it. The read-through is the same thing, it's a truly thrilling experience in every sense, difficult, stressful, but thrilling. When you play the scenes with other characters in the play, they come to life, more often in the read-through more than anything, and sometimes it doesn't happen on the stage, as it should.

The rehearsal period is, at times, a working-through and back to what you may have done in the beginning instinctively, perfect; it is a time of sublime showing off with no restrictions—"see how good I am? Watch me! See how I bring to life these thoughts on a page. I'm a full- blown recognizable person, one you care about and feel for, on every level of life." It can be magical, much the same way as a musician brings life to the world of sound.

From the notes on a printed score, the pianist takes you on a journey of sweeping passion, by the sheer artistry of his forgotten technique, so to speak. Technique doesn't even enter into it, and it should be there from the very beginning, so that you can forget it.

Same thing with acting, and then to that the heart of the moment is what the composer has set down in the score in whatever century he or she was in. The read-through, and then the harp of the emotion. If I may say, it has lived. An amalgam of mind, heart, musical sensibility, and entering in to a zone of sense and interpretation that uniquely you and no other, save the marrying of the composer's intent, and your own.

That is why, in my opinion, every great artist playing the same work makes it sublimely his or her interpretation, and you know who is playing without being told. Much as in singing, when you hear Caruso, you hear the quality of the sound, as no other can produce, the hallmark of any inescapable artistry and vocal prowess that is embedded in their vocal chords—that's acting at its most thrilling, something embedded somewhere in the mind, body, and the sensory mechanism of the actor.

This is the furthest thing from automatic pilot that some actors take for creative acting; they do it the same in this play as they did in the last play, and then they do the same movie over and over again, and then all of a sudden you think, "my God, doesn't this person know how to act?"

Anyway, we moved en masse to New York to start rehearsals, and then Michael Kidd hired all the dancers for the show and singers for the chorus. It so happens that among the dancers, there is one who is name Valerie Harper. Well, I guess you remember Valerie Harper with Mary Tyler Moore; she went on to fame and fortune as either Mary Tyler Moore's roommate or just part of the show. You'll never know how one's career comes to fruition, when and whatever takes place, and why one achieves a career over another, equally talented person—kismet, belief system, right place, right time, who knows?

Since I was playing the juvenile lead, who happened to be Mexican and who was an oil rigger in the play, the sidekick of the leading man, I decided to speak with a Mexican accent all day long, so that people would think that I was Mexican. It got to the point that everywhere I went, people would ask me where I was from in Mexico.

One actor, H.F. Greene, is a very special human being. He has as big a heart as any living human being, generous, funny, and one of those people who ultimately becomes one of your closest and dearest friends. He happened to play the Mexican cafeteria owner. So, one day he asked me at rehearsal how long I'd been in the U.S., I laughed and I thanked him for the compliment, using my Toledo, Ohio accent.

I can still see him laughing in, what to me was, a congratulatory way. He was to become, as I said, one of my closest and dearest friends. There are very few in life who really achieve this, and he was to become a great part of my life. H.F. was a man seemingly untouched by the ruthlessness that can happen in the business to many actors when they've reached the peak of their dreams. His attitude was a love of life, no matter in what color it should itself be presented. His basic habit was to get a Broadway show for six or seven months or more, then take off and collect unemployment for the rest of the year.

He loved to gamble, and he did so with the greatest of style. He never had trouble in getting a new show, and he always auditioned with the same sixteen measures of a song, he looked rather like the typical Mexican man, always tanned, with a black handlebar mustache, and he laughed off every challenge. To say he loved life is an understatement. He knew he had a heart condition, and he kept saying to me, "Listen, I'm living on borrowed time anyway."

He became for me, during rehearsal, another eye, watching what I did and then giving me the notes on my work, should it be necessary. His criticism was always honest, straightforward, and constructive, and he was a huge fan of my work and he talked about me all over town in rather glowing terms.

Lucille was a consummate artist and, for her, during this terrible time of divorce with Desi, she kept a shrewd eye on every phase of the production, and when cuts had to be made, she did so with great care, making sure you understood it was nothing personal, but only for the good of the overall production.

Lucy founded the whole show from the very, very beginning, no outside help. She was not only the star of the show, but its producer, and time came for the other town openings.

It was a time when Broadway shows took to the road to sharpen and shape every phase of the show, from new songs, new scenes, cuts, wherever they were needed, she knew how to listen and to take advice from those that she trusted and who had ultimately the final end of the product, which is a marvelous show. She made every call of what was in and what was out. The first out-of-town tryout was in Philadelphia, and for me it was an adventure that I shall never forget.

The purpose of an out-of-town adventure, or taking the show on the road as it's called, was to make sure the sets, the costumes, the lights, and the sounds were perfect. That huge orchestra supporting the score of the show and the songs—you can hear what's going to work and what isn't going to work, and she had the final say on everything.

I can't begin to explain the exhilarating state of mind and body, the chance to constantly change what, I felt, I could do better, conventionally within the form, and structurally, so that it fit into the whole, as a mosaic became a part of the whole. The show became a new show for me almost every night, I performed it being a gypsy at heart.

When I wasn't working or rehearsing, I was out scouring the city, finding new places to shop, to eat, to search out the architecture, the cultural life of each city that I went to, and H.F. would always go with me. If he wasn't working on his own scenes, he would accompany me. I loved buying presents for those that I cared about, and gifts to others was, in reality, a way of pleasing myself. To be and feel the joy it gave others, really gave me greater joy.

Harold Pinter

At one point I happened to be working on a movie entitled *Bill and Ted's Excellent Adventure*. We were shooting in Tempe, Arizona. I brought my family to Tempe to meet Keanu Reeves and Alex Winter, Bill and Ted's perspective characters. They were gracious and everybody had such a good time and as for my assessment, they were perfect for the roles they were to play—charming and that kind of zany quality of the very young it; worked perfectly and they were lucky as producers to have these two wonderful actors.

Toward the end of the shooting. I got a call from my agents, and the conversation went something like this: "Hi, clifford, how's it going? I answered," It's been going very well and we are almost finished shooting the movie."

The agent replied, "I hear it's fascinating particularly with the young, who may make this into a cult show, that wouldn't be more supportive or nicer!" The agent said, "Listen the reason for this call other than to tell you about the good vibes about Bill and Ted's is to tell you I got a call from the Richard Rogers office. Eddie Blom in fact asked me about you and when did I think you would be finished with the movie."

I told the agent, "I thought we'd be finished within a week or so. Why?" The agent said, "He asked me, didn't Clifford do Harold Pinter's play entitled Old Times? I told him that you had done it a few years ago."

Eddie Balaam answered, "Well, Harold Pinter has asked to meet with him and discuss some things that he had in mind."

I nearly jumped out of my chair, actually my skin, as I considered Harold Pinter a genius and probably the greatest living author of our times. I told my agent it was wonderful working on Bill and Ted's Excellent Adventure and the cast was in great form.

So, I was looking forward to having a meeting with Harold Pinter and no one knew exactly what he had in mind. There is something sad about the ending of a project, particularly when it was a great experience. I knew in my gut that this would be a movie that had great following. We hadn't finished the last scene of the movie, and so a small crew of actors and two or three crew specific to the final scene, we were all flown to Rome. I was put up in the most sumptuous hotel and I think it was called the Savoy, right in the heart of Rome close to the Vatican. It seemed Dino De Laurentis spared no expense, as his daughter was the actual producer and he wanted to do well by her.

The editor had been working simultaneously, cutting the movie as we were shooting so that by the time we flew back to Los Angeles, we had moved quickly so that the movie would not be difficult to finish cutting.

I was more than anxious to meet Harold Pinter. When I got home I checked my messages and found I had an urgent call from Mr. Rogers office, Eddie Blom in fact. The message stated that "Could I meet with Harold Pinter at the Beverly Hills Hotel on Friday at noon for lunch?" This was Wednesday, so I had a little jet lag but anticipation and excitement was very high. Friday couldn't come fast enough.

At that time I had a wonderful old Cadillac convertible, beautiful to look at and it ran superbly. I put the top down and rode to the Beverly Hills Hotel that Friday. The valet guys were only too glad to display it on the entrance level at the hotel, good image for the hotel. The Beverly Hills Hotel structurally is and was the image of the 30s. Grand Spanish buildings within elegant entrance, port cochere. Fancy entrance, the works. It was pink in color with huge green leaves painted on the walls with birds of paradise added.

As I strode into the lobby, there was Harold Pinter and his wife Lady Antonia Fraser, an incredible writer herself, a powerhouse team. We went in to the Polo lounge for lunch.

Everyone knew who they were, and assumed I was somebody since I was with them, so they were more than deferential and seated us at a table next to the window that looked out onto the sumptuous gardens. Sumptuous to say the least. The image of glamorous Hollywood in all its glory.

Drinks were ordered and since I don't really drink, I ordered a soda to their scotches. I should've had a glass of wine to calm me down, but then I really wasn't thinking about anything except being with them, and I didn't want to chance the thought of feeling ill and unable to hold intelligent conversations with them.

Harold Pinter began to explain to me that he hadn't been on the stage for 17 years and that he was unsure that he would be able to complete the work necessary for "old times" to be as effective as he had envisioned it when he originally wrote it.

He asked me, did I have any difficulty in playing a role, and if so what were the difficult spots? I said to him that the character of Deely was so beautifully written that in playing the character, it ultimately became easily understood that somewhere in his mind the images of past events evidenced themselves to the constant repetition of his conversation with the two women. He looked at me and said, "Do you think you would care to stand by for me in case I felt I couldn't do justice to the play and to the other actors? You see that Liv Ullman, the Swedish actress, will be playing a crucial role and I would want to be an authentic asset to the production."

I said to him, "I don't believe you could be anything but an asse, After all this is a play you have written, no matter how long ago it occurred, you wrote it and it will all come back to you as to why you wrote to play to begin with!"

He said to me, "You're very kind but I still have doubts and I hope you will be there to critique me should it be necessary."

I said, "I hardly think that will be necessary but truly I am very flattered that you would choose me to standby for you." I was more than flattered because here was this genius of the writer expressing doubts as to whether he would be able to fulfill the requirements of a play he wrote albeit many years ago.

I don't believe anybody ever really loses the genesis of their writing or their performance. It's just a question of polish, and simply doing it, in the repetition of something, like a muscle, it responds to what we knew and have known basically.

Lunch and dinner after about 2 1/2 hours and we agreed to meet next week to begin rehearsals. We started to rehearse at a rented studio for about ten days and then we moved into the theater where Liv Ullman joined us for full rehearsals.

There is that peculiar quality when a writer assumes the role in the play that he has written that brings a rather different quality to the work—not necessarily what I would have done, but different and equally as valid.

Little by little Harold Pinter began to lose that subjective criticism of himself and the work. It is a difficult play to come off, and one which demands of the audience to think and be a full partner in the journey of this play. In a way it has to do with memory, even though at times the memory may be false but no less important. And somewhere in the recesses of the mind the memory takes over in a very imaginative way and conveys a deeper meaning than just what the word implies.

The rehearsal. A very thrilling time, and on our day off, Harold Pinter and his wife invited me to go to the beach for an alfresco lunch. It was more than fascinating to hear them speak to each other in a way that was extraordinarily educational of thoughts that ran through their minds. The questions they posed gave me a wonderful opportunity to experience how these people thought and what occupied their minds.

Fortunately I was able to join in, because they discussed

subjects that were truly interesting to me and have always been on my mind and I'm sorry to say there were very few people with whom one could discuss the questions that they posit. It was like watching two brilliant tennis players battling back and forth with ideas of enormous scope.

We then returned to the rehearsal hall and theater to set the play for opening night. In my bones I knew it was going to be brilliant, but I felt a little leery that the California audience would be tested to sustain their involvement in this brilliant play. They could easily. It is just a question of would they, as California and Hollywood had particularly interesting and intelligent people. It was just a question as to whether they would be willing to work through the play and, of course, witness Harold Pinter's return to the stage.

After each night of the performance of the play, he and I would discuss how I thought the play went and how his performance was received. I assured him it was brilliant, and it was after all why shouldn't it be as you wrote. He knew exactly what he wanted to convey as the actor and writer of what he had written. We have very few actors who write in the scope of Harold Pinter. Liv Ullman was brilliant, as well as the other actors whose names at the moment I have forgotten, I'm sorry to say. It was a highly successful run by anybody's standards and the privilege of standing by for Harold Pinter was just that, a privilege. Later on, who knew that he would be given the Nobel Prize for literature a well deserved honor.

A Way to Share

You see, now that I have money, after so many years of not having anything, it had a special meaning for me, it was a way in which to share with others the things that I thought were beautiful. Watching the person receiving the gift was possibly more thrilling for me than it was for them. There is something about a gift and when it is given that speaks to the deepest need in me to be appreciated, if not loved, and to be moved.

I had to check and make sure that I gave the gift that I thought would most please them and would be at the heart of their appreciation. If I'm honest with myself, I can freely admit an almost holy search for the truth of what I am playing. Nothing mattered to me, save the success of bringing to life what I had in my mind's eye, and at times, not easy working with any director who is insecure of his or her own concept of the character.

I've always felt that more directors try to live through the actors they hire, and then some even give line readings to the actor, a very fine line had to be walked with such directors, and thank God it was not so with me.

Michael Kidd or Lucy, who could if she chose, alter any concept I had, she was extraordinarily generous. She wanted everyone to be at their very best, and not afraid to bring to life what you had in your mind's eye. Some stars are very difficult about letting an actor come to full fruition, some feel that it takes away from their sterling qualities, or whatever they felt like, and that was not Lucy. Lucy wanted you at your best. Much like the idea of your playing tennis, to play with somebody much better than you. Lucy had so much invested in Wildcat, and not just money, which was considerable, but high on the list was reputation; Lucy fail? Never. Wildcat was a huge show in many respects. In one of the scenes, Michael had constructed scenery, so as to build an oil derrick right in front of the audience's eyes. The audience was mesmerized, when in previews, they saw it. It was a rough period, as most shows are in the beginning, scenes rewritten, songs cut, the play and the whole tightened into the end of the first act. Keith Andes, the male lead opposite Lucy, and I had a beautiful duet, but it was cut because it impeded the flow of the play, and it took the storyline in a whole new direction. Lucy knew that audiences were coming to see her, and not a play about wildcatting oil.

The struggle in the play was not to present a play with music, but a musical that had its emphasis on Lucy discovering oil, and Lucy in a romantic situation that ensues with, at the same time, the discovery of oil. I had other songs, as well as a duet with Lucy's sister in the play. The sister, as written by Richard Nash, had a physical disability, I think it was a club foot, and Hank, my character, convinces her not to let anything stand in her way, that she could dance if she wanted to, and the song became a duet entitled "One Day, We Dance," a touching and very human scene that points out Lucy's protective care of her sister, showing Lucy as a loving and caring sister, and it worked. As previews commenced, it became clear that this had to be a show all about Lucy. Audiences were not interested in anything else, they had seen and grown up with "I Love Lucy" and wanted an extension of the "I Love Lucy" show as a wildcatter.

It was six weeks of grueling rehearsal, cuts, rewrites, and everything else to keep Lucy in the spotlight, as much as possible. There was some great dancing and some marvelous songs that Cy Colman had written, "Hey, Look Me Over" being one of them. Lucy didn't have much of a voice, but she knew how to sell a song. I remember she worked incessantly on her voice, it had a rough quality to it. At one point she needed oxygen to keep going, and she worked harder than anyone I had every known, and we all did so, we worked harder than we thought we could.

When we got to New York, after Philadelphia, the weather was brutal, unbelievably freezing cold, and everyone came down with something. One day, coming into the stage door at the Alvin, as it was called, The Alvin Theatre, the doorman said to me, "Clifford, Ms. Ball wants to see you, so go to her dressing room first, before you go to yours." Her dressing room had been redone with all the amenities, draperies, bed, chaise lounge, wall paper, paint, rugs, I thought to myself, "I wonder what she wants, what can she say to me at this late date? Fire me? Jesus, I hope not." I was fighting a bad cold and all I wanted to do was go to my dressing room, make tea, and prepare for the evening performance.

I remember walking down the hallway, rather exhausted and even trepidatious, and as I walked down the hall, I came to her door, which had a huge star on it, and below was Lucy's name. I knocked, and from within the room came her voice saying, "Who is it?"

I said, "It's me Lucy—Clifford."

"Come in," was all she said, nothing more. I walked into the room and she was sitting at the makeup table, and her hair was being fixed by the hairdresser. She had the usual cigarette in her mouth and she was trying to put on makeup, ten things at once, that was Lucy.

"Yes," I said, "You wanted to see me?"

She turned to me and she said, "Clifford, you see that box on the chaise lounge?"

I said, "Yes." "Well, take it and get out of here."

Well, I was half stunned, take it and get out of here?

"Take it and get out of here?" I said.

"Yes, you heard me. Get up to your room and take care of yourself."

Well, I breathed a sigh of relief, and I took the box, it was huge. What could it be? I went up to my dressing room, took off this rather ratty overcoat that I had, and I hung it on the hanger, and then I went to the box and opened it. Well, I think nearly went through the floor. Inside that box was a beautiful navy blue double-breasted overcoat, and the label on it said Vicuna, handcrafted in Italy. I just stared at it for the longest time, and as I unfolded the coat an envelope fell to the floor.

I picked it up, opened it, and in Lucy's hand it said, "Get rid of that thing you call an overcoat, stay warm. Love, Lucy."

Well, if you don't know what Vicuna is, it's about the most luxurious lightweight wool you will ever feel, soft, warm as toast, double-breasted, and I looked like a million bucks in it, and the coat cost damn near as much, I was completely floored.

She'd always been warm to me, and most complimentary about my work, but this was so completely unexpected and generous beyond belief, and this coat must've cost a fortune. I put it on immediately and looked at myself in the mirror. The color was perfect, beautiful, and it made me look like a movie star, the kid from Toledo, Ohio in a show with Lucy, getting co-star billing on Broadway. I'm working with the world's greatest and most famous star, and, in some respects, I hadn't fully realized how great and famous she really was.

When you're very young, and rather full of yourself, there's a lot you don't know, and you're apt to take things for granted.

We finally arrived at opening night, and I had sent for my parents to be at the opening night with my brothers and their wives, it was a great, if nervous, opening night for me.

Lucy on Broadway, and one of the most popular of Broadway stars ever, and there was also this tune, "Hey, Look Me Over," it resonated with the public, and if not a smashing success, it was so with the audience, and Lucy knew that long before anyone else: it's the people who count, who buy the tickets, and who come more than once.

It was a success at the box office, and with the crowds

every night at the stage door, it was just unbelievably breath taking. And now comes the amazing part. Not before or since has a show closed and then opened at a later date. Maybe some historian will correct me on that score, but we played for nine months, then closed for Lucy to take a break and rest, and then after two and a half months, we opened with a huge box office advance.

Lucy on Broadway, to the great public acclaim, was amazing. People loved her beyond belief, and in my opinion, that's what makes a star, the people who buy the tickets. Desi came around during the previews, and I'm sure he gave some input into the show, he wanted it to succeed, and I knew Lucy loved him deeply, but just couldn't come to grips with past history between them. Desi was considered a great producer, and together they changed TV sitcoms to what it is today.

I think it can be said that they invented the three-camera mode of shooting, and shooting a sitcom is still the way most TV shows are done.

I decided to give the cast a party at my West Side apartment, and I invited Lucy. I never imagined that she would come, but she did. Not only did she show up, but she brought along a few friends and cases of different things, liquor, beer, everything, generous beyond belief, always, she loved the members of her cast, they were her family.

The party lasted until 3 a.m., and then she regaled us with other stories about Hollywood and all her past experiences, both in Hollywood and New York. It was really a thrilling evening, and to hear about her early experiences in New York, on Broadway, well that was just history coming to life.

Lucy was devoted to her mother Dee Dee, and, naturally, she came, and added to the stories of her chaperoning her daughter into Hollywood, into New York, in the early years for Lucy.

It wasn't particularly kind, and like so many others, she didn't quite know what to expect, and the studios didn't quite know how to handle Lucy.

Consequently, she was put into the movies that weren't truly suited to her extraordinary gifts, it was television, and her writers, who knew what was the perfect fit for Lucy, and the sitcom became "I Love Lucy," and the rest is history. She was one of the very first women executives who headed an entire studio, and she turned out to be a great businesswoman.

I believe, in many ways, Desi's death took a great deal out of her, and she spent the rest of her life looking for some kind of peace. The only thing that took her out of one reality and into another, was the work, and that is exactly what she did.

One of the saddest comments I think I've ever heard a star of her magnitude make, was when she was on "The Dick Cavett Show" one evening, which was a very popular show, very much like Johnny Carson, but slightly different, and still with celebrities, and no bigger ones than Lucy. I was watching it and she looked wonderful, and then she said, "I used to be on television." Well, it can be said, she made television like no other, the world waited weekly for the "I Love Lucy" show, and her, in America and all over the world, yea, she used to be on television.

When you work with someone, no matter who in my case, I'm sorry to say that I never truly knew who Lucy really was, and the label "major star" doesn't really tell you much. America is addicted to hype, and also believes in fantasy that some of the stars, in essence, come up with, and more often than not, the end of the publicity agents and the rest of it, but a garbled mess was the ensuing problem.

In fact, it was the same thing as in the case of Marilyn Monroe. Icons, yes, but like icons, Byzantine icons, frescos, they are, in reality, one-dimensional. Take a good look at most of the icons, they tell you very little of what truly beats at the heart of the image at hand. In fairness, most don't know who they are, really are, and maybe that's why they fade in the public eye. Many are remembered by images on films, paintings, photographs, memorabilia of every kind, and the major problem for any actor, is to continually test and extend their talents to find the outer limits of what is real, and what is fantasy, and perhaps at a point in which they come together, but I'm not sure. I think, maybe, they do.

If you experience a person, a star, of that quality, the icon quality, more often than not, the public can only see that person in that particular venue, and so it's a constant struggle to disabuse them of the category. A true actor is one possessed of many phases of their talent, and that is often confusing to the producers and directors: "He acts, she sings, he dances, she dances, which? Why not all?" I found it necessary to continually switch career choices, not to confound, but not to let anyone put me in a box, and say, "oh yes, he or she is this."

To that, and my next period, which was a Broadway show I nearly missed doing, it happened just like this. My agent had submitted me for a project entitled The Aspern Papers. It was an adaptation of a Henry James novel, adapted for the stage by Sir Michael Redgrave, and was to be directed by a marvelous actor/director, Margaret Webster, the daughter of Dame May Whitty and Ben Webster, a legendary couple.

On the day of the audition, I had a difficult night sleeping, and I overslept, so I dressed very quickly. This was when I lived on West 46th Street, and the theatre was on 44th, I believe. So, I dressed quickly, and since I lived close to the theatre, I ran all the way, only to arrive at the stage door, just as everyone was getting their coats on, or ready to leave.

The stage manager, Jose Vega, said, "Well, well, well, Clifford. I see you've just arrived, and maybe too late." He looked at me, kind of smiled or smirked—he's a great guy, we were friends, and he said, "Listen, wait here, and I'll see if they would care to see you"—they meaning Margaret Webster, Sir Michael Redgrave, and Morris Evans, the star of the play. I waited nervously in the wings, cursing myself, "How could you be so stupid to jeopardize a chance for a new Broadway play, specifically one with a legendary cast, and one which included Wendy Hiller, the original Eliza Doolittle in Shaw's play "Pygmalion," Françoise Rosay, a very famous French actress, and, naturally, Morris Evans, whose Hamlet was legendary, having been directed by Margaret Webster in an uncut version on Broadway, and also that it was an adaptation by Sir Michael Redgrave of the Redgrave family.

As far as Broadway or the acting world is concerned, there couldn't be any higher recommendation. I saw Jose Vega coming toward me, and there was no expression on his face, that I could detect, and it was either, "go home, you're too late," or "okay, they'll see you."

Well, thank God it was the latter. I breathed a sigh of relief, and I am, to say the least, always nervous of auditions, and I mean nervous beyond belief, and even more so today, partly because I've never been late, which could be taken as, "he doesn't really care." Well, that couldn't be further from the truth. Naturally, as I was near broke and needed a job, needed it badly, I walked down to the stage, and what greeted me was Ms. Webster's voice, "good afternoon Mr. David," in this very clipped English accent, which is not an accent at all, it's her voice, but she was right, because it was 12:15 p.m.

I said to her, "I am so deeply sorry to be late, please forgive me. And I thank you for giving me this opportunity to read for you."

Ms. Webster said, "Mr. Vega will read with you. Let's do the discovery scene." This was a scene in which the Italian manservant, Pasquale, to Mr. Evans, discovers a trunk full of love letters written by Lord Byron to the aging Venetian aristocratic woman, who once was a femme fatale, and that happened to be Françoise Rosay.

Now, she was wheelchair bound, and attended to by her niece, Ms. Hiller. The object was to steal these letters, and give them to Maurice Evans, for whatever purpose. In truth, Pasquale is a thief, hired by Maurice, to find these valuable love letters and, ostensibly, publish them. Well, I got about ten lines into the scene, and as I was very dramatically uncovering the chest with these letters, and it was a behavior seemingly, to me, perfect for this kind of very dramatic Italian flourish, almost operatic, "here they are!" and I was coming to terms with a grand gesture like a bull-fighter, as I was exposing the trunk containing the valued and prized love letters, long lost to the world, and Mr. Evans was bound and determined to have them, well, there came a clear voice from the auditorium, "that'll be enough Mr. David."

My heart sank, and I made a move to head for the stage

door, slinking out, again,

Ms. Webster said, "Where are you going Mr. David?" and I looked and stopped, I was rather shocked.

This voice said, "Maurice, will you go on stage and stand next to Mr. David?" It all happened so very quickly, I wasn't sure what was going on. Maurice came onto the stage, stood right next to me, and the next thing I heard was Ms. Webster's voice, saying, "thank you, Mr. David. Rehearsals begin Monday morning at ten sharp." The sharp was absolutely evident, don't fuck up, don't be late.

Jose looked at me with a shit-eating grin, and said to me, "Congratulations, you think you could make it?" As I write this, I'm shaking from the memory of it all, and I'm trying to breathe deeply, just as if I had escaped being guillotined.

Later that day, as I was walking down 5th Avenue, right in front of Saks 5th Avenue, I heard a voice, distinctly English voice, calling out, "Mr. David! Mr. David!" I turned around only to see Sir Michael Redgrave running up to me saying, and I was completely taken by surprise, when he grabbed my hand, shook it firmly, saying, "Mr. David, I am so glad you are doing my play."

I mumbled something like, "I'm very grateful to you for having me a part of your play, and thank you for casting me in it."

Well, I can't explain how it makes one feel, and me in particular, but a great actor, such as Sir Michael Redgrave, would take the time and the effort to run up and congratulate an actor, a fellow actor who wasn't particularly well-known. I was well-known in the industry, but certainly not in the outer world, and feeling that rare expressed by American actors. This may have something to do with English actors, in particular, who, to my mind, are more generous to the actors they admire. It is perhaps a tradition of actors, and acting, I'm less threatened by other actors.

I, more often than not, am taken for English, which I'm

not totally sure why, but it is no secret I admire greatly so many English actors who take great risks in their work, particularly in Shakespeare and in the classics. The only things that come to my mind, is that every time I audition, or deal, with an English person whose background is English, they're more likely to know what they want, or see in you exactly what they need and say, "Yes, thank you, that's it, rehearsal begin....," just as Ms. Webster said, "rehearsals begin Monday at ten sharp."

No equivocating, or extraordinary situations saying, "Oh, well, we have to look at—", no, none of that at all, they're very professional, and courteous to boot. It seems, no casting by committee, that has been my experience. Does it have to do with four hundred years in the theatre that make a difference? History?

Cult of Personality

The cult of personality acting exists in the English theatre, and movies as well, but it seems to me less so, and more to see how far they can take their talent against straight works of drama.

Monday morning at ten sharp, I actually got there at 9:30, rehearsals began on the stage, and everyone, including Olympia Dukakis, a friend and a marvelous actress, was there, along with Augusta Merighi, an Italian actress who played the maid, or the housekeeper, a typical Italian mama, to say the least, it was a wonderful cast. The first read-through went very well, and rehearsals were a marvelous experience.

The ladies Ms. Hiller and Madame Rosay were strong and forceful, and you had to be on your toes because they were really strong actors, and if you let down your guard, you could be wiped off the stage.

We did our try-outs out of town, again, in Philadelphia at The Walnut Theatre, one of the most beautiful older theatres in the world. It's beautiful because the inside is all wood, and it was a very intimate theatre. Ms. Webster, Peggy to her friends—and I, were lucky enough to be counted among them as we got to know each other over the rehearsal period—she was a staunch advocate of my work. So much so, that she gave me the working copy of her Shakespeare photo that she was working on, and it was the photo for Hamlet, with the hope that I would play Hamlet in London, under her direction—but more of that later. Little did I know that she had to fend off the two strong ladies from firing me.

What occasioned this animosity had to do with the staging of the play, because at one point in the play, I was placed upstage in a dimly lit stairwell, listening to everyone's conversations, taking measure of how and when I was to steal the love letters. Bear in mind, I was a thief posing as a manservant to Mr. Evans. The girls are not too happy about that.

During the last preview in Philadelphia, the stage manager, here we go once again, said to me, "Mr. David, Ms. Hiller would like you to come to her dressing room." Well, I thought maybe she's going to wish me a great performance, or a good evening, something that one actor would say to another, and maybe she would tell me that she loved my work, although I couldn't believe that.

By the way, the girls were a very strong group of ladies, the two of them, and Peggy said to me, "the girls have been at me to fire you," and with that she handed me a beautiful small box with playing cards in it, as she knew that I loved playing solitaire. I played it every night before going on, as I was in the dressing room preparing.

As always, I had a cold, and I tried to calm myself by drinking hot tea. The performance that night was spectacularly exciting, and I got a huge applause on my exit of the scene, much to, I'm sure, the displeasure of the ladies.

So, the next night, I went to the theatre full of myself, cold and all, only to be greeted by the doorman with, "Mr. David, Ms. Hiller would like to see you in her dressing room before you go to your dressing room."

Once again, news from the doorman, only this time I was sure there wouldn't be a Vicuna coat waiting for me. I knock on Ms. Hiller's door, and "Come in," came this rather plumy English voice.

I went in, and the conversation went like this, "How are you Mr. David?"

"Getting better from this cold or flu, thank you. I don't want to get too close to you, because I might give it to you, and I wouldn't want that. I was on my way to myY dressing room when the doorman said you want to see me."

"Yes," came this plumy voice again. She said, "Mr. David, I've known many gentleman's gentleman, and they do not behave as you do, and as you are doing in this play, you make yourself too important. Gentleman's gentleman fade into the background and are rarely heard from. Do you get my meaning?"

"Yes indeed, I do, Ms. Hiller. However, you see, I am, in reality, a thief, and an Italian thief at that. One who is out to steal the love letters of Lord Byron to your aunt. Now, if you'll excuse me, I'm not feeling well and I need to go to my dressing room. Good evening, and I wish you a very pleasant play," and with that went out the door, only to steal the evenings performance once again, in a scene in which Pasquale steals the love letters, and again, to an applause.

Peggy came up to my room, and she said, "Did the old girls get to you?"

"Yes," I said.

"Well, just keep doing what you're doing," and with that, she gave me a kiss on my cheek, "see you tomorrow, you don't need a rehearsal, take care of that cold. I loved her for that, and I had a sense that she had been protecting me, all the while, from the girls, as she chose to call them. Margaret Webster was a woman of extraordinary talents, she was born for the theatre, it was in her bones. She came from an equally extraordinary acting family, and some may remember her mother, Dame May Whitty, from movie fame. When she went back to England, after the play closed, we ran for a season, and then after that I went to England to prepare myself to play Hamlet.

I had studied her uncut Hamlet version as close to the original, Shakespeare, as possible. She had written it in preparation for a Penguin Books publication, and for what I had hoped to be my English debut. When I got to England, I went to Christ Church, which is a section, I think north of London, a part of it, a suburb like, where she lived, and then we were going to go to Windsor.

A Strange Experience

It was a strange experience to come into contact with a part of England that came close to approximating the Castle Elsinore in Denmark. Windsor seemed a fortress to me, and the strangeness of the experience was heightened by a sense within me, that I had been in this region long before, in another life, in another time.

In fact, after that, I just happened to be in a gathering of English actors and celebrities at a party held in a 12th Century manor house in the country, I believe it was in Kent, and during the evenings festivities, a woman who was rather well-known in London as a mystic, as I was only to learn later, came over and sat next to me. She introduced herself as a friend of the hostess, and the conversation went something like this, "Are you enjoying your visit to England?"

"Yes," I said, "immensely."

She said, "Have you found some things familiar?"

Well, I was rather puzzled, and I looked at her, and I said, "Yes, but I'm not sure why."

She looked at me, straight in my eyes, very dead serious, and she said, "You've been here before."

"No," I said, "I was just here with Ms. Webster to obtain a green card, and permission by British Equity to play Hamlet in the West End, after doing a tryout. First, I have to try out in South Africa, in Johannesburg, and then, hopefully, London."

She looked more Russian than English, her dark hair was pulled back in a bun, much like how ballerina's are, her face elongated, oval, with blue eyes, and skin of the whitest quality, almost having no color in her cheeks. She wore a Chinese Empress's robe, unbelievably striking in color and design, with large full sleeves, embroidered with dragons, and an electric blue background, and she used the sleeves as one would a muff, to keep her hands warm, so that when she withdrew them from their voluminous sleeves, and gently took both my hands in hers, they were hot to the touch.

The woman, in a very flat tone of voice, said, "No, you have been here before. You find that, at times, you will cross the street for some unknown reason, to avoid meeting someone you may or may not like to talk to, or with to see or speak with," basically to avoid, is what she was saying.

She went on, "I see you don't drink."

"No," I said, "just wine perhaps, a little bit, or maybe some champagne at dinnertime, very little."

"No, I mean real alcohol," she said, "scotch or bourbon."

I began to feel a little uncomfortable, with her blue eyes staring deep into mine, not threateningly, but steady as she spoke to me.

I said, "It makes me ill, and whisky makes my stomach turn, and in fact, it hurts."

She said, "Did you ever ask yourself why?"

"No," I said, "Really, it just makes me ill to drink, and I don't like the feeling it gives me."

"And what about crossing the street to avoid someone you don't wish to speak with or acknowledge?"

There was a long silence, and then I said, "how do you know that?"

She continued to ask, "do you find it difficult to memorize all the lines in Hamlet?"

"No," I said, "Now that you mention it, now that you've reminded me, I really have found it quite easy. I love the language, it's precise, full-blooded, and Shakespeare strikes at the heart of expression, like no other writer now or since."

She said, "I'm going to tell you something that you can either believe or not."

I started to sweat, not knowing where this was going to

lead.

"The reason you can't tolerate whiskey, or strong alcohol, is that you were an actor in the 17th century, in England, on the brink of great stardom, but you were a notorious drunk, and actor managers of the day were afraid to hire you, and you crossed the street to avoid the essence of people who remind you of the past period's acquaintances. The shame you felt was a consuming one, and that is the reason you can't physically tolerate alcohol. Eventually you ran away and drank yourself to death. You see, you haven't completed your journey as yet."

She held my hand tightly and said, "I wish you every great success, and Peggy has great hopes for you. I'm sure you won't disappoint her," and with that, she got up and swept away to another part of the huge hall-like living room, with a wood-burning fireplace and all.

I have an imagination that runs wild as it is, and this set me around the bend. I can't drink strong alcohol, and I do avoid people, for the most part, feeling they know something about me that I am unwilling to divulge. I prefer to be under the radar, so the speak, and for most of my life I've had the strangest feeling of abandonment, partly I can't really tell you why.

When fall is in the air, very often, I have dreams of being in England, and the feeling is one of inescapable sadness, and oftentimes I'd wake up weeping, and, honestly, no sense of where I was, or wrong. I'm sure these sensations are not particular to me, and I'm sure any number of people have, if not identical, but similar experiences throughout their lives.

Somehow, we're all connected in a way that would be difficult to prove, but nevertheless, there is a connection: six degrees of separation. I do not ordinarily give in to mysticism or new age spirituality, as is too often filled with bogus ideas and con artists, and I won't defend my supposition or sensory feeling, but somehow, there is nothing in the mind that does not come from the senses, Gassendi is the author of that thought. An inexplicable way should perhaps remain inexplicable.

The Betsy

When I co-stared with Laurence Olivier in The Betsy in 1978, on one occasion I happened to ask him if he remembered Margaret Webster and me, and the relationship with the British Equities denial of my doing Hamlet in London, in the West End.

He looked at me, and responded by saying, "I wondered when you were going to ask me about Peggy's mentioning you for Hamlet in her production in the West End."

"I didn't want you to presume I would ask you about the denial, as you were president of British Equity at the time."

He responded by telling me that at any one time, only 2% of British actors were working, and that an American playing Hamlet in a British production was not going to be permitted.

Now, English actors work in America, and in American productions, both in film and stage, so I said to him, "What's the difference?"

"That's something that Actor's Equity has to rule on," was his reply.

"It doesn't seem equitable, or fair," I said, "It should be reciprocal, tit-for-tat, so to speak."

"Ah, well, that's all in the past," he said.

I looked at him and said, "Not for me." I said, "It was a missed opportunity to see an American actor, to see and to hear, if he could pull off, and perhaps bring to life, a different interpretation, still connected to Shakespeare's intent.

A case in point, somewhere along the way, is the soliloquy, "Oh, that this too, too solid flesh would melt," in the actual written manuscript of 1603.

This is what I said to him, "The word sullied was written in the text, and someone in favor of solid as a metaphor for melt, replaced the much more literate sullied for solid, and in my opinion, it cheapens the overall quality of the play. Surely, Shakespeare's meaning, and the text, is preferable to any other person's viewpoint. This is, to some, convenient substitution to make the text understandable to the ground-lings. Shakespeare is as much a being of elegant language, as is the plot."

Olivier looked at me after a long pause, and he said, "Point well taken. I'm sorry, but it couldn't be helped; at that particular time British Equity was fighting for its life, for sub-sidies by Parliament."

Once again, politics rears it ugly head. We're forever to be ruled by inept and political politicians, and it should seem so, since nothing ever really changes. The idea of change is difficult for most people, and a long battle has to take place before real change can take place.

Olivier's claim is a convenient one, in light of the ac-tor's equity of British Equity and American Equity, whereas American Equity permits English to work in every field of entertainment. Is it because we revere British theatre, and all things English in the theatre and the films?

Anyway, The Betsy was a great experience for me, work-ing with Sir Laurence, and Dan Petrie did a marvelous job. Even though it did not become a box office smash, it dealt with the car industry in a timely fashion, the goings-on in Detroit. At one point, I had a scene with Olivier, in which he accuses me of corrupting his son, the implicit action and line is sexual blackmail. When we started the scene, Sir Laurence had assumed that he had the upper hand, well, to the con-trary, I had other ideas, including blackmail and a takeover of the company.

We started the scene and Dan watched very astutely and carefully, he wanted to see how the scene would play. I came on rather soft-spoken and intellectual, and at the council, in the crucial part of the scene, I opened up with a startling on-slaught of this line of questioning him.

Sir Laurence stopped and looked at me in a way that was more surprised than annoyed, and after a long pause he said, "Ah, so we're going to play it that way, are we?"

I said, "There are many ways to play it, but I felt that this was the proper way, given who I am in this affair and scene," and the cameras stopped, and Dan Petrie said, "cut!"

We looked around and, once you've been in the business for a while, you learn quickly how important the entire crew is, how vital they are to the success of the movie, and in a very subtle way, they judge you and your work, though nothing overtly said, but they let you know their approval or disapproval, and thank God it was the former, they approved. You can feel the sudden change in their demeanor; it becomes respectful, without being obsequious. I had scored a hit, and to Dan's satisfaction, I'm sure.

Olivier said, "May we begin again?"

And Dan said, "of course Larry. Just give me a little bit of time to set up the lights and a new focus for the camera, I want close-ups between the two of you."

Strength in an Actor: Olivier

Sir Laurence is, or was, a notorious scene-stealer, and I was having none of it. Strength in an actor is a subtle thing, not a sledgehammer approach, and deep down I could feel Olivier's surprise and, somewhat, pleasure of what the scene could be off the written page, however deep down, an animal level territorial prowess, high stakes stuff, but that's what makes acting something particularly great, when you are playing with a world class actor.

At that time, Olivier mastered all forms of acting, and the old Olivier came onto the scene, this was no walkthrough, and it was not a walk in the park attitude. One must remember Olivier's exemplary performance of Richard III, he came on the scene and it changed immeasurably.

I think Olivier usually rested between scenes, and now he chose to talk to me, ready to discuss the Hamlet affair. I confess, I'm not big on confrontation, nor am I inclined to just lie down and be walked over, but there are a few opportunities to bring to life the kind of power, particularly against a legend.

In the final analysis, movies are a director's medium, and what one sees on the screen, the final product, is up to the director and the editor.

Movies are sold according to the star power of the lead actors, and the money is riding on that name, and the movie is, more often than not, made on bankability of the star. Some are wonderful actors, but few can, what is called, "open" a movie. The definition, in movie terms, open means that a bank will fund a movie because of the star involved, and the assumption is that a major star will draw big box office results, money in other words. It was, after all, a business, no matter what many of us, as actors, hope for.

Other considerations, for my part, are when the story is

a great one, and the actors chosen are more than capable, along with a director of insight and sensitivity, then the final product can be exceptional. Take, for instance, "Citizen Kane," beautifully cast, the story is intriguing, and Orson Welles as star and director brought to the screen a truly great film. Historically, it had a very difficult time being released. William Randolph Hearst brought to bear the full power of his influence on other powers in Hollywood not to release it, so it had to be shelved. The movie was, essentially, about him and his relationship with Marion Davies. Marion Davies, of course, was his mistress, and I won't go into any of the details that have been written about ad infinitum.

In San Simeon, California, his castle, on the pacific coast, is legendary, and it is an extraordinary feat of architecture and imagination, mountains were moved to accomplish and accommodate a perfect site to view the entire coast. In scope, it can rival any palace in the world, and it was filled with antiques from all over the world, the ultimate in luxury and excess.

It is legendary that the Baronial Hall in San Simeon could seat an enormous number of people. Movie stars would come up for the weekend to play, swim, and dine elegantly, with the exception of the mandatory bottles of ketchup. Mr. Hearst wanted ketchup on the table, every five feet or so. The table stretched from one end of the hall to the other, some thirty feet long, of this incredible dinning hall. I think it can be said that the power in those who possess it by virtue of money, corporate holdings, or social position, is often expressed subliminally, or overtly by some, of those particular echelon— think of King Henry VIII, and his not so subtle display of power over his wives. If they disgraced or displeased him in some way, some were beheaded, others banished, and all of this in search of a male heir, the power of establishment on his own, of course, religion. He confiscated land, money, and everything that would fill his coffers to solidify his power, and add to that his fondness for composing music for songs and dances.

In the theatre, there are various ways to exhibit power, often insinuating themselves into a story, over a writer's work. It is a wonder that few products and few productions, whether in the theatre or in the movies, ever comes to life exactly as the writer expresses it, or has written it, or there is at least a faithful adaptation of their story brought to life. Product by committee is the antithesis of a product brought to fruition by an author, a single person. To name a couple, Ingmar Bergman and Fellini, these are the rare exceptions.

On a Clear Day

I'm reminded of a musical I did on Broadway, created by Alan Lerner of My Fair Lady fame, with Fritz Loewe. The musical was an enormous success, and Alan, in my opinion, was one of the few great lyricists in the theatre. He was also a man who could, very much, do as he pleased; he created a play called On A Clear Day You Can See Forever," which dealt with the phenomenon of Bridey Murphy. It was a story of a woman who remembers having lived in another century, and all the attendant relationships that ensued. On A Clear Day is a story of such a woman, and I believe it was the 18th century where she had an affair with a young Lord by the name of Edward Moncrief, a torrid love affair at that. The psychiatrist is intrigued by her recall, and attempts to go further into the 18th century life at that time. Naturally, he falls in love with her, and then it becomes a tug-of- war between Edward Moncrief, the 18th century lover, and the modern psychiatrist. Burton Lane wrote the music, Burton Lane of "Brigadoon" fame.

And now begins the fun.

Alan was a man of seemingly independent means and could do, pretty much, what he wanted to do. I remember auditioning for Alan, Burton Lane, and Bobby Lewis for the role of Edward Moncrief; I always seemed to be cast in English roles at that time, not that I was doing anything consciously, English accents just always came easily to me.

Herb Ross was the choreographer, and more of him later. The offer for me to play Lord Moncrief came immediately, and Louis Jourdan was contracted to play the psychiatrist, and the wonderful and charming Barbara Harris was to play Melinda, the duo-life heroine. Barbara had a unique quality, one of extraordinary dramatic and comic ability; she was also given, at times, exotic behavior, and erotic behavior, never affecting her work, but at times her personal life. I remember one time she decided to be a salesperson at Macy's, and I'm not sure if it were for financial reasons or if it were just a whim, I suspect the latter.

She had a very independent mind, to say the least, and, frankly, I adored her and loved playing the scenes with her. At one point in rehearsal, we decided to rehearse the seduction scene in Lord Moncrief's studio, and Herbert Ross decided that he really wanted to direct. He wanted to try his hand at anything that would come along and be amenable to being directed by him.

Big mistake. Barbara and I knew instinctively what the scene needed, it was a disrobing of sorts, Barbara as Daisy, down to her skiff, and I was almost bare-chested. Picture this, a large theatre, the Mark Hellinger, empty, as everyone had gone to lunch, and a bare stage. Herby was in the audience, seemingly giving us his input, not needed, I may add, but not wanting to offend him, we listened. However, Barbara and I knew what needed to be done in order to make this scene come to life, really come to life. Every song, in my opinion, in a musical, must come from the point at which words fail to express the subtext and the intent of the song, and the real reason for the scene. In the middle of this scene, Sir Lord Edward Moncrief, sings one of the most beautiful songs of any musical, it was called "She Wasn't You," which expresses his love for her and the ultimate in physical desire.

In the middle of all of this, this rehearsal while we were by ourselves doing it in the theatre, Bobby Lewis, the director of the musical, comes into the theatre, and asks, "What's going on here?"

I waited for Herby to speak up, but nothing came from him, and so after a long silence, I spoke up and said, "Bobby, I want to try and do this scene as a seduction, with Barbara, and as an improvisation," and I knew that Bobby knew exactly what was going on. He gave Herby a withering look, since Herby was the choreographer and he was the director, it was a very uncomfortable situation, I can tell you.

I could immediately see the quality of who Herby was, and is, and the lack of willingness to speak up as to what really was going on, I lost respect for him instantly, not that he much cared, I'm sure.

Such manipulation in the theatre is frequent, and some careers are made by duplicitous behavior, and some people succeed by whatever means possible, and whatever is comfortable for them, whatever the state of denial to the actual situation may be. I am uncomfortable, even as I write this, and one must remember that this is my viewpoint.

Speak-Singing

Louis Jourdan was hired for the run of the play, and Louis doesn't sing very well, but he did as he did in Gigi, he speak-sings, as does many actors, such as Rex Harrison in My Fair Lady. So, Burton wrote the songs with that in mind, and rehearsals went on, and after a grueling pace, Clear Day was a huge show. It had huge sets, magnificent costumes, and glorious music, with some of the most sparkling lyrics in all of Broadway musicals. Alan was a perfectionist.

I happened to be in the same hotel as Alan and Burton Lane, and many times I would hear Alan and Burton in heated discussions late at night, because my room was just below theirs. The subject was Louis and his inability to really sing these songs. We would rehearse during the day, and Alan would rewrite scenes for Louis to go to his hotel and study the new material, or so he thought. Now comes the hard part.

Unknown to Louis, John Cullum, a wonderful actor, was hired, it seems, to study the same role, the same material, and occasionally I would see him somewhere backstage listening to the days' rehearsal. Well, you can guess what happened, Burton wanted to get rid of Louis and replace him with John, and the real problem was the chemistry between Barbara and Louis was so superb, it was one that couldn't be matched, and remember, Louis was an international star, and we had a huge advance due to Louis, Alan, Burton Lane, and, not the least, as I said, Louis Jourdan of "Gigi" fame. The charm that Louis had was unmatchable, it didn't matter one wit that he couldn't sing. You could feel the romance of these two characters flood across the orchestra, into the auditorium.

Speaking of the orchestra pit, it was an extraordinary something to watch, the Mark Hellinger is a huge theatre. Alan couldn't decide from one day to the next how he wanted the orchestra pit to be, so the rows in the front of the theatre were removed to make room for the huge orchestra. But the next day, he didn't like it, so the rows were put back in, and the orchestra was placed partially under the stage. It went from one extreme to the next, and the cost was staggering, but Alan wanted what he wanted, and in Boston he would disappear for days at a time.

He not only had a hotel suite in Boston, but he also had his yacht anchored in the Charles River, where he would spend nights sleeping, or reworking, or whatever else he does.

Dr. Feelgood

Now comes another part of this story, enter a man by the name of Dr. Max Jacobson, also known as Dr. Feelgood. One incident I will never forget happened on the opening day of opening night, and we were rehearsing, preparing for the night. Louis had the flu, Barbara had the flu, and I had the flu.

Alan came in from his yacht and saw the situation, and well, Dr. Max was summoned, and one by one we were hauled into an outer office, which served as the doctor's office. Max brought out this huge cylindrical tube with a large needle at the end of it, and it had been filled with an array of colorful liquids, much like a barber's pole; yellow, green, and blue, all in various layers. I believe there was a drink that looked like that at one time.

Anyway, when I went in, I could hardly speak. I was saving my voice to get through the evening's opening, because "She Wasn't You" was a very large song, high in the tessitura, as it's called, and beautiful long legato lines that had to be just right, otherwise forget it, the song would never be what it could be, so, I had to get through this evening's opening performance.

When I presented myself to him, without a word, he lifted my shirt, grabbed the muscles around my waist, wiped the spot where the needle was to enter with the alcohol to sterilize it, then he anesthetized it, and then plunged this huge needle into the spot that had been sterilized and cleaned, whereupon he looked at his watch, after having stuck me with his thing, counting the seconds, and finally all the liquid had been drained into my flesh, and he said, "Well, that should do it." It was like I was transported into another world, I couldn't believe what was happening, it seemed like I was flying. My voice was as clear as a bell, strong, clear, and absolutely brilliant. What a miracle this guy had brought. Listen, your guess is as good as mine, as to what that concoction contained, all I knew, was that I felt like a million bucks, and I performed that afternoon incredibly. However, the real surprise, came when Abe Feder, the lighting designer, came into "Max's Den," as I called it, and Abe, who is virtually blind with coke-bottle-lens', thick beyond belief, was in the middle of trying to finish the lighting for the show for opening night. I was in the process of getting myself put together, when Abe walked in, and the dialogue went something like this:

Max: How long have you been nearly blind?

Abe: Most of my life.

Max: So you can't see a thing without them?

Abe: No.

Max pulled out a phone book and asked Abe to read the names in the phonebook, with his glasses on. Even with his glasses on, it was very difficult for Abe to read.

Max: How do you see the lights?

Abe: That I can see.

Max: Alright then.

And with that, he opened Abe's shirt, and all the while, as he'd been talking, he'd been filling another cylinder, large, with a new needle, of course, and filled it with all the colors of the rainbow, like mine was. He looked at Abe and cleaned the spot where the needle was to go in, and he grabbed the muscles around his waist, the same as he had done for me, and he injected this concoction. Abe looked bewildered, and Max was looking at his watch as he was injecting the liquid into Abe's body, and when he finished he said, "there. Now, take your glasses off." Abe took his glasses off and looked around the room.

You could see his face, there is no describing what it looked like. It was like somebody had just touched him on the forehead and his face was alight with wonder. Max handed him the phonebook and said, "read this phonebook without your glasses."

Abe let out a scream, "I can see! I can see perfectly without my glasses!," and with that he ran out saying, "I have to finish the lighting for the show, how long will this last?"

Max said, "it'll last long enough, a few hours, maybe more."

Abe ran from the room yelling all kinds of the directions, practically relighting the entire show. Dr. Max Jacobson was the man who had attended to JFK and his back problems. That night at the opening in the Colonial Theatre in Boston, something happened, as the day had been filled with surprises, to say the least, but an event happened, one I will never forget. Abe finished the lighting, and the stage was set for the opening night at the show. The Colonial had very little backstage room, so most of the sets had to be flown high into the wings and the ceiling, and it was huge, it went all the way up, because that was the only room.

There was a stage and one walk space, but no back place to put anything. Everything had to be flown into the ceiling, and it was lifted by thick, heavy chains that had been hoisted and secured, and as the sets and scenes changed, the stagehands would lower the sets onto the stage, into the back, and in the dark. We would then take our place "magically," as it would seem to be, and it created, all of a sudden, a studio, my studio, by using a platform that was set with huge windows, at the back of the platform, a chaise lounge, curtains, draperies, and beautiful, rich fabrics everywhere, just swathed in the most expensive material that anybody could buy, and the impression was a large studio for painting, with light streaming through the window, flooding the set, it was staggeringly beautiful.

"Not Yet"

Barbara and I were standing in the wings, waiting to go on, and there was a doorway that led onto the stage, barely four feet between the entrance and the set, which had been hung in the ceiling by these huge chains.

Well, for some unknown reason, instead of going onto the stage, I grabbed Barbara by the elbow and said to her, "not yet." I pulled her close to me, back into the doorway, and she looked startled as to what I was doing, but as I did that, the chains holding onto the set broke, and the set came crashing down onto the stage, breaking the entire set apart. Now, had we been standing there, it would've crushed us both to a pulp, and after it happened, Barbara looked at me and said, "did you know that?"

I said, "I had no idea. I just felt something. I just wanted to move back, for no discernible reason," freakish, to say the least. The set was in shambles, the windows partially destroyed, everything a mess, and we still had to go on and do the scene, and I was to sing "She Wasn't You," the most beautiful song in the show.

My mind was racing, and all I could think about, was how grateful I was that we hadn't been killed, both of us, inwardly I was just shaken, but with a rush of adrenaline, we created a crackling scene, full of life, grateful to be alive, and a thunderous applause as cap to the scene.

Alan came running backstage in a state of shock and gratitude, and he kept asking, "Are you all right? Are you all right? Are you sure you're all right?" It was just a miracle that we got through it.

The show itself lasted four hours, and then the next day, we saw cuts in the academy scene, costumes and all, and at one enormous cost. I had a black velvet costume studded with diamonds and buttons and various stones, it must have cost a fortune, and Freddy Wittop was the designer, no expense was spared. My costume was sewed for another scene, and that night Alan sent a bottle of champagne to my room with a beautiful note, and let me tell you, I needed it. The crew was deeply apologetic and the cast truly concerned.

The next day, tired as we were, we rehearsed with all the cuts to be inserted that evening. Additions to dialogues were changed and virtually handed to us right before going out, we did it by the seat of our pants, it seemed, don't think, just do. The show was immeasurably better and tighter, and the Boston audience was marvelous, and showed it by a fabulous applause. It was just breathtaking, raw enthusiasm for the show. Louis was marvelous with Barbara, and as Alan had planned, the audience wanted them to be together, and that's another thing for star power.

Louis was not the greatest actor in the world, but he had that special something that can't be manufactured or duplicated. As good as John was, there wasn't that charm, that charisma, that magic, so to speak. Burton Lane had managed to ease Louis out, and I'm not sure Louis had cared, as he had a run-of-the-play contract, so he was paid in full for the nine months that we ran. He went off to France to be with his friend, and fellow star, Boille, of movie fame, and Louis' wife, who's a charming woman, and I'm sure a great help to Louis, but before being given notice, I visited him often, though never letting on what I knew was taking place in the background.

I felt he needed an ally, just as a fellow actor, and no one can know what it is like to be let go, fired, I guess would be the cruel word, and in my opinion, it was the show's loss, as most of the advanced sales in New York had dried up, and it can be called a victory for Burton Lane. Burton was not a bad man at all, but he decided, in the middle of things, that he wanted to hear the music over the lyrics, and so Alan gave in.

I'm not sure just how well Alan really was, during this period, as Dr. Max Jacobson was in constant attendance. Anyone who's ever created a show, and a huge one at that, knows just what kind of toll that takes, on you and everyone around you. Read what the composer and the producer's have to say about the creation of West Side Story, the pieces have to fit together perfectly, and at that time, Clear Day had cost several million dollars, and we were the highest priced Broadway show at that time. Imagine, the highest priced ticket at that time, was $11.95, laughable by today's standards, but not back then. Clear Day was a magnificently beautiful show, from every aspect, a visual and stunning delight. It should be reworked and brought back as a Broadway show, and even now as Broadway is so inundated, in my opinion, with so much lesser works, none with this kind of magnificence. When it came time to do the movie, I met with the powers-that-be at Paramount, and Howard Koch was then head of the studio. I was told I could be in the movie, however Barbara Streisand wanted to sing "She Wasn't You" as "He Wasn't You." Well, I thanked them all, but no thank you. If I couldn't do my song, I didn't want to do it.

Star Power

Star power, once again, rears its head, and whichever way you want to take it, it's not always the best solution, in my opinion. As great a singer as Barbara Streisand is, it didn't have the same impact in the movie, the movie itself lacked what the Broadway production had. Look, not being on the money side of movies and productions, I have, and had, only one thing in mind: how do you create something great that will go down in history and become a mainstay in the lexicon of a play or a musical? Why have the works of Shakespeare remained constant? Every actor with confidence has tried his hand at Hamlet.

How many productions of Hamlet have been chronicled over the years? It's hard to tell. Look, Oklahoma, Carousel, Guys and Dolls, and West Side Story, to name just a few that are standards in the repertoire, Clear Day could've been just such a musical. Look again at My Fair Lady, Burton Lane wrote a great score, and some of it required singing, and singing well, without being miked, as today's singers are, it was hard, and most of the voices lack real power, today, and would have no ability to really sustain eight performances per week, that is the schedule, eight shows a week.

I'm not sure how the voices of today fare, what with the screaming, and the belting high into the upper range of the singing, most of them burn themselves out in a matter of months. I guess there will always be enough people to replace those who fall by the wayside, and there are always more who will come along, but at what price: Rex, to say the least. The idea of studying is a thing of the past.

Dancers are the most disciplined of the performers. You see, the body will quickly give out with sustained abuse, as in Joseph and the Amazing Technicolor Dreamcoat, the dancers had to dance on a stage with wall-to-wall carpet, beautiful to look at, but when the dancers had to turn, the body went one way, and the knees went another, and they were anchored in the spot, so that it twisted the knee, due to the carpets, thus causing a turning to the knee. Performers had to be protected from those who don't have to perform, and constantly practicing.

The rehearsals for On A Clear Day were long and hard, and Alan, as I said, stayed on the boat for several days, and when he emerged he added huge changes to the book. Essentially, he was constantly improving the scenes, and the manner in which the songs would have a launching pad, so to speak. Mr. Richard Rogers always said, when I worked with him on The Boys From Syracuse and I Married An Angel, he said, "A song should only come into a scene when words fail to express the intent of the scene," in other words when words don't add to the scene, it's the music. Think of Billy Bigelow in Carousel, when Billy sings "My Little Girl," it's heartbreaking, as it should be. The Boys From Syracuse was something else, and it hadn't been done for years, and one of the producers was a young guy, not terribly experienced in producing, but he had the idea it could be done fairly reasonable Off- Broadway.

Well, when push came to shove, all the money needed to rehearse, for costumes, sets, musical score, and anything else, was not funded by him, and he didn't have the ability to raise that kind of money, so Mr. Rogers had to step in and put up the major amount so that we could open the show. Christopher Hewett was the director, and he was so perfect for this particular show, that he managed to pull it all together, and the cast was superb, every actor was perfectly suited to the roles they were to play. Ellen Hanley, Julienne Marie, Cathryn "Skipper" Damon, and Karen Morrow rounded out the female leads, and Stuart Damon and I played the twins. The music was absolutely beautiful and the rehearsals went along well, and the thing that makes a cast really good, is the respect and the real affection that they show each other, no back-biting, no jealousy, a very happy experience to say the least.

Hammering the Shoes

When we got into the 54th Street Theatre to start previews, everyone was amazed at the sets and the costumes, however, the shoes, a very important part of the whole picture, left a lot to be desired. You see, my sandals, in particular, were, to put it mildly, rotten, hard as cardboard and practically un-wearable. Remember, we had eight shows a week, and we had to do four shows on the weekend, two on Saturday and two on Sunday, back to back, with only a half an hour between shows for us to grab a piece of bread or something, and if your feet were killing you because your shoes were wrong, there was no way to correct that little matter. So, at the dress rehearsal before opening night, the sandals that were giving me so much trouble, they were so stiff, hard as thick card-board, as I said, that I could hardly get them on. I went to the stagehands, got a hammer, because I knew a hammer was needed, and then I proceeded to take the sandals off, sat down on the concrete steps, and proceeded to pound them to a pulp with this hammer.

This young producer was absolutely horrified, and the cast was in stitches watching me demolishing these sandals. He screamed at me, "What are you doing?" I yelled back at him, "making these things wearable! I don't have any bun-ions or calluses on my feet, and I don't intend or plan on having them now!" and as I said, the cast could hardly get through the dress rehearsal without looking at my feet and laughing through the dialogue. The shoes, of course, became far more comfortable, so we finally opened to the cream of New York audiences. Limousines were lined up and down the street, all the way to 9th Avenue, because the theatre was on 54th Street between 9th and 10th Avenue. People were dressed to the nines, and there must have been millions of dollars worth of jewels worn by the women. Men in tux's, ladies in gowns and furs, it was a very, very ritzy crowd. The next day, Janet Maslin, who was one of the major critics in New York, wrote a glowing review, and capped it with the phrase, and I have never forgotten this, "Oh joy, oh rapture, oh Rodgers and Hart!"

Needless to say, you couldn't get a ticket to this show, rarely does a cast sparkle with talent in every actor, as it did in The Boys From Syracuse. Every review was glowing, with praise for each of us, and Mr. Rodgers was absolutely thrilled. When writing about my experience in the entertainment world, so much comes out of left field, so to speak, my association with Mr. Rodgers grew into his wanting me to do one of his shows called I Married An Angel.

There was no book for the show, and as Mr. Rodgers wanted to include it in his library, he arranged to have it done in Palm Beach, Florida at the Royal Poinciana Playhouse, Elaine Stritch, Taina Elg, and I played the leads. I had never been to Florida and, loving the sun as I do, it felt like an ideal vacation. Rehearsals went along smoothly with Mr. Rodgers rewriting certain parts of the play and the music, and bringing to it a complete form. The pianist in the pit was a woman by the name of Natalie, who had been with Mr. Rodgers for years; she was employed by him constantly, and she did many of his previous shows. She could play pretty much anything that he wrote, in any way that he liked it, and she knew exactly what he wanted.

At one point in the rehearsal, Natalie, seated at the piano in the pit, we heard this voice waft up after a very long rehearsal, she let out a comment that made us all double over with laughter, she could be heard saying, "My God, this show is wall-to-wall music! We need to hear a scene, or two!"

Mr. Rodgers was not offended, he merely said, "Natalie, I'm working on it."

Elaine had a habit of having a glass of champagne before going on stage, and she said, "Clifford, have a glass of champagne, it'll make the work go easy on you," and she was right, but if I had more than one glass I would've fallen down.

You see, as I said before, I can't really drink, and at one point I decided I was going to have a party for the cast, and we took over this entirely huge rooming house, very close to the beach, where everybody stayed. It was cheap and it made you feel like you were in a movie, it was wonderful.

Mr. Rodgers came, as did Eddie Blum, his right-hand man, and a grand piano appeared, it was brought out, and

Mr. Rodgers sat down and began to play one great song after another, all from his very own shows; he was an incredible musician.

Worth Avenue

I had only heard of the legendary Worth Avenue in Palm Beach, the shopping ground of the very rich and famous, and one day Mr. Rodgers secretary called me on my day off and said, "Mr. Rodgers would like to know if you could have lunch with him this afternoon."

My God, would I? Could I? Are you crazy, you must be nuts, of course. I didn't say that, but I was deeply flattered to be invited by one of the truly great legends in musical theatre and in theatre per se.

His chauffeur picked me up that afternoon, and we went to lunch somewhere in the heart of Worth Avenue, we ate at a very chic and, needless to say, famous and expensive, and I mean expensive, restaurant. After lunch we walked the street of Worth Avenue, looking at all the stores filled with every imaginable luxury item, open sesame to the treasures of the rich and the exclusive Palm Beach crowd.

When we got back to my apartment that afternoon, and after a very successful run at the Poinciana Playhouse, once again, Mr. Rodgers invited me out to lunch, and this time it was in New York City.

He couldn't have been kinder or nicer to me, and he wanted me to see newly erected Lincoln Center Complex, the Metropolitan Opera House, the Avery Fisher Concert Hall, and the New York State Theatre. After we had been walking around all of these incredible theatres, we stood in front of the New York State Theatre, and then Mr. Rodgers said to me, "Well Clifford, we brought the whore uptown." Fortunately I knew the reference to that statement.

Musical Theatre: "The Whore"

You see, in the early days, musical theatre was known when it was downtown on 14th Street, where it was known as "the whore." Crowds were needed to have legitimized the musical theatre as an art form, which of course it was, and through his efforts and many others.

But he, primarily, spearheaded the idea that musical theatre was an art form. Particularly in his hands, his partner, Lorenz Hart, and Oscar Hammerstein, their contribution to the musical theatre was, and is, groundbreaking. It no longer was just a bevy of pretty girls, but they saw to it that the new musicals had a story line, and in fact Carousel was adapted from the play Liliom by Ferenc Molnár. Musicals under his oversight began to include adaptations from great literature, it no longer relied on sketches and various fill-in skits. Sophistication and a deeper source of inspiration came, and after all, Mr. Rodgers and others in the musical theatre were steeped in classical music. Take for instance Leonard Bernstein, one of America's great musicians, composer, and pianist, musicals began to demand performers as well as writers.

Musicians were needed to seek out the very best in every phase of production, singers were classically trained in order to negotiate some of the music, such as Carousel, West Side Story, Clear Day, Sweeney Todd, 1776, and so many more. Stephen Sondheim says, and has said in the past, that he doesn't much care for trained voices, but if I may interpret that statement, he doesn't care for, what I call, plumy voices, when the voice is all and the lyrics incidental, but if you listen carefully to all of his music, you better know how to sing, or you could lose your voice, and constantly be at the throat doctors. Green Finch and Linnet Bird is no walk in the park for any soprano, and a young one at that. I believe one must follow their own instincts and path, and stop turning yourself into a pretzel to suit the occasion. Pinza, the great opera star, the basso cantante, who is probably one of the greats in all of opera, sang in "South Pacific" by Mr. Rodgers and Oscar Hammerstein, and he really had to sing as well as act. His Don Giovanni by Mozart is legendary, it seems everybody has two professions in this world, their day job, and the know-it-all in the arts—whether it's acting, singing, or dancing.

And Unemployment

Lest you think I went from one show to another, let me disabuse you of that notion, there were many long periods of no work, and occasional standing in line at the unemployment office, and when I wasn't doing a show I was constantly studying acting, singing lessons, or dance, you name it, I did it. I can honestly say that satisfaction with my own work was rare, and I was a very severe critic of my own work, and I could always see what was needed, at times too much so.

Some voices are very mature at the very beginning, little work, fully formed, and from day one they were built by sheer health and energy. Witness Enrico Caruso, one of the great voices of any century, listen to his earliest recordings, he built that voice, granted the quality was there at the very beginning, but not the full-bodied sound, and the expression in his great years. One of the greatest all Bulgarian sopranos was told as a young lady that she had a sweet party voice. Her mother was her first teacher, and she sang light opera until a teacher, by the name of Dr. Bratt, told her that the reason her voice was small was that the chords didn't come together, adduct, is the proper word.

When he worked with her on the physical aspect of the vocal chords, her voice grew exponentially into one of the most spectacular voices in all of history, particularly in Wagner. It went beyond huge, she could sing easily over a hundred pieces in the orchestra with no trouble at all, take time to listen to these great voices, and when you really think about it, I have, on a daily basis, come to the conclusion that energy is the springboard to creativity, one has to have will and energy to maniacally quest for, what to some may seem, madness or unattainable.